YOGA, Truth, & The Real Fountain of Youth
(zeroth edition)

Damon Givehand

Copyright © 2018 Damon Givehand

All rights reserved.

ISBN-13:9781796322460

DEDICATION

This is dedicated to the Love of a whole, unconquered, and harmonious Humanity.

TABLE OF CONTENTS

Preface	vii
Acknowledgments	xi
Introduction	xiii

PART 1
REMOVING LIES & INSPIRING CHURCH

It's Real	3
Truth As Is, Not As Wished	4
3 Major Modern Mistakes	7
What Goes Around Comes Back Around	13
Light In A Dark Age	15
The Trustworthiest	18
Have Church & Get Pregnant Por Favor	19
A Whisper From The Past	23
The Bible & The Fountain	24
The Bible & Yoga Fit Like Hand-In-Glove	25
Breadcrumbs From Our GGs	28

PART 2
THE FOUNTAIN OF YOUTH & GETTING KNOCKED UP

The Fountain	39
You & I	41
The Terms Youth & Yoga	42
The th Suffix of You	45
It's In Ewe	47

Ewe & Eye	49
The Brain's Uterus: As Above	52
The Ewe-Taurus	55
The Living Fountain Revealed	57

PART 3
INTRACOURSE: LOOKING BACKWARD & FORWARD

Elaborating Yoga, Youth, & Truth In Review	63
The Fountain Of Youth	67
Now What? What's Next?	69
The Practical Earthly Things We Can All Do	71
9 Divine Suggestions	74
Final Words (for now)	88
APPENDIX A — Getting Quiet So We Can Hear When We Listen	93
APPENDIX B — How to Read The Bible	95
APPENDIX C — Fasting	97
APPENDIX D — The Power of Breathing on Purpose	101
APPENDIX E — Detox, Cleanse, Maintain	105
APPENDIX F — 3 Key Sutra Transliterations And Translations	109
APPENDIX G — Adequate Quality Rest Recommendations	111
APPENDIX H — The Prospect of Health	113
APPENDIX I — The 8 Limbs of Yoga	115
About The Author	119

♦ PREFACE ♦

"Je n'ai fait celle-ci plus longue que parce que je n'ai pas eu le loisir de la faire plus courte." ~ Blaise Pascal

TRANSLATION: I have made this longer than usual because I haven't had time to make it shorter.

WHO IS THIS BOOK WRITTEN FOR?
Are you committed to Truth, or are you committed to finding confirmation for your previously held beliefs? Since nothing can enter into a mind that's closed, the mind must be open to receive Truth and to allow Light to shine in. Truth also requires us to dig and to make connections that may not have been made before, which often means a lonely road for the pioneering dot-connector, calling for courage and unshakeable confidence. And, TRUTH requires HONESTY (with self especially), a painful price most aren't willing to pay because it leaves us openly exposed with all our shortcomings, misperceptions, and false beliefs — none of us likes to feel like we've been fooled and we like it even less to admit to others that we've been fooled.

Yet, for those of us ready and willing to pay that price of pure and brutal self-honesty, pursuing Truth no matter where it takes us, even when it means we have to put foot in mouth admitting that we were wrong about some things we once fervently believed in and were convinced were true, the return on investment far exceeds anything we might imagine in a favorable way, especially in learning the Truth about the Fountain of Youth (and that's Truth with a capital T). That said, this book is written for individuals interested in True Truth and willing to pay that painful price of GROWTH; those who have learned to thrive off such pain, embracing its discomfort because it hurts so good; those who know the growing pain is temporary and a necessary effect of an expanding consciousness; those who know that knowledge of self is the supreme knowledge of all. That's who this book is for! (HUE)MAN, KNOW THYSELF!

YOGA, TRUTH, & THE REAL FOUNTAIN OF YOUTH

The Real Fountain of Youth and the associated content contained herein represent an observable and verifiable discovery with abundant practical value. What's written on the following pages is not a rhetorical discourse bent on dazzling those who happen upon this with fascinating conjecture and plausible theories we might all "like to believe" and "wish" were true. The Fountain of Youth is not a make-believe fantasy! It IS REAL as you will see.

Because I felt this information so vital for the healing of people sooner rather than later, it was more important to release this info and get a fresh conversation started asap than to let my ego get in the way with wanting to come across perfectly polished on the page by repeated and exhaustive edits and rewrites, for fear of being criticized or challenged. Time is of the essence!

Due to the nature and freshness of this content, criticism and challenge is unavoidable, inescapable, and inevitable (especially by forces that oppose the Liberty of Souls), yet easily overcome because the observable proof is visible for all to see with their own eyes, so there's no need to take my word on blind faith for anything. On the other hand, I welcome criticism and feedback, as it will help me make needed improvements on the forthcoming revised and edited 2nd edition. Please send constructive feedback to damongivehand.com/contact.html.

The following pages are virtually raw and uncut. Thus, I'm calling this first edition the "zeroth" edition. That said, I apologize in advance for any loose ends I might forget or neglect to tie up, etc. I will revise this publication in the near future, but for now, as I said, I just wanted to do my part in contributing to the conversation without hesitation or delay so that we may begin to heal sooner and more quickly.

I have not published this as a scholarly work with the intent of competing or arguing with other scholars and researchers OR with the desire to impress people with how deep this information and the connections made might seem. I have published this to share what is probably the most important discovery of our time, and to show the ease with which anyone can conduct their own investigation into this subject matter. The Truth is right in front of us and does not ask us to take another researcher's word for anything. All we must learn to do is look and listen with eyes and ears prepared to see and hear, then use our own reasoning faculties to draw our own conclusions. I'm not asking you to take my word for anything, my only hope is that you let all your previously held convictions go and read the following pages with an open mind and heart.

To demonstrate that this type of research doesn't cost a penny and is literally at our fingertips as long as we have internet access and sufficient desire to know the Truth, I've used some simple online resources. For word origins and root meanings, my primary tool for this book has been etymonline.com, which should be assumed throughout this book unless otherwise noted. I recall from my college days at FAMU, under the tutelage of Dr. Juanita Brooks in the 90s, the relevant neuroanatomical terms, but for anyone lacking such educational experience, a quick google search will turn up countless websites with stunning visuals on brain anatomy (which I utilized on occasion for review). I used Patañjali's Yoga Sūtras (which I've been studying enthusiastically since 2010) and The Bible (King James Version), and for anyone who doesn't already own copies of these, both are easily accessed online for free. And finally, I've leaned on the spontaneity of my mind to allow flashes of light to stir certain curiosities in me whose questions have consistently led to innumerable, unexpected mini-epiphanies while researching, gathering, contemplating, and organizing this work.

This information is not hidden, unless we consider it hidden in plain sight. To know the Truth, all it really costs us is time and effort — the time to look and the effort to see — and that is where the true value is... in how we spend our time. TIME IS INFINITELY MORE VALUABLE THAN MONEY. We can make money back if we lose it, but time lost is gone forever. In fact, time shouldn't be spent, it should only be invested. Since you have more time than money, INVEST YOUR TIME WISELY and read every page in this book carefully. Look and see!

I sincerely hope you and others use the ideas and presentation I share here as a springboard into your own voyage deep within and throughout the wondrous rabbit hole. I hope to inspire you to also share your discoveries so that we may ALL become more aware, knowledgeable, and upright, while growing wiser and more graceful, individually and as a whole, into a unified and harmonious people once again. Sharing is caring! And we are in this together!!!

Before we begin, you are forewarned that the topic we are about to discuss, what you are about to read, goes way deeper than these pages allow and have space for, and we are not even scratching the surface of the scratch that scratches the surface. This book does its best to steer clear of conjecture and wild conclusions, adhering to the three criteria of correct perception as articulated in Patañjali's Yoga Sūtras, and is written with the express intent of being "relatively" short (considering all that "could" be said/included), while packing fresh connections never published or seen before. To that end, there is also some liberal use of repetition, especially in Part 2 (with a little in Part 3), intentionally repeating certain points and concepts to help new ideas stick better while increasing the efficiency with which the bigger picture can be grasped wholly.

The brevity of this zeroth edition is for the convenience of the reader who's pressed for time. In light of this book's curtness, you are encouraged to research any of these ideas further as they pique your unique curiosities, and align them with the chakras, kundalini, the christos, etcetera, which I deliberately do not go into in this book because of another project. Only YOU have the exact combination of questions that YOU have, that must be answered to YOUR own satisfaction during YOUR lifetime. That said, a curiosity I hope to pique in you regards what and where the REAL Fountain of Youth actually and literally is.

♦ ACKNOWLEDGMENTS ♦

My deepest thanks goes to Kiala Givehand, my soul mate, best friend, lover, and wife, who has stood alongside me and supported me through the thickest and thinnest of times. And to ALL my teachers over the years.

Damon Givehand

♦ INTRODUCTION ♦

"On résiste à l'invasion des armées; on ne résiste pas à l'invasion des idées." ~Victor Hugo

Where is the Fountain of Youth? If I was to tell you in your ear where the fountain of youth is, you'd hear "...the fountain of youth is in you and I." I'd be sharing a profound truth with you in the most direct and explicit way, yet the words uttered would not convey what you are about to read, in even the minutest way; not because the words "...the fountain of youth is in you and I" aren't clear, or because I violated some grammatical rule for prepositions, but because you, the hearer, have been trained to hear in one predominant and predictable way. By the end of this book you are going to hear "the fountain of youth is in you and I" in an entirely new way, and you are going to "get it." Yet, if you tell others, they won't get it for the same reason you are unable to get it at this point in the reading.

This book requires an open mind and a willingness to think far different than we were trained and conditioned to think in school. As a result of our education (which includes TV, radio, movies, and media), many erroneous beliefs have been so deeply ingrained in us that we are likely to experience resistance to many of the ideas shared in this book. I'm telling you this up front so that you may have a greater chance of noticing when resistance rears itself, increasing the likelihood you'll be able to overcome the tendency we have to be and remain close-minded. Unless genuinely curious, the ego tends to want to close the mind off to ideas it doesn't already believe in, even when previously held beliefs are baseless and incorrect, so I spend a significant amount of time in the Introduction and Part 1 laying a foundation intended to inspire curiosity and open minds so that Light may enter.

You may have heard a quote that goes something like "Nothing can stop an idea whose time has come" without knowing where the quote itself comes from, and that it wasn't originally communicated in English. The opening quote of this section is the original quote, by the French poet Victor Hugo, and can be literally translated as: One resists the invasion of armies; one does not resist the invasion of ideas. With the literal translation of this quote, neither the power nor accuracy gets lost. And while the translation offered in the first sentence of this paragraph is powerful, much is potentially lost because the author's original words are not directly translated. Yoga, Truth, And The Real Fountain of Youth shares many potent ideas, however, whether or not these ideas' times have come remains to be seen (but I believe so). Nonetheless, an invasion of enlightening ideas is underway!

THE LIVING WORD
Language can protect and preserve Truth over the ages. While each generation is born and eventually dies, the words they use to communicate ideas and stories with each other while alive continue to live carrying those ideas from generation to generation without dying as long as the words are spoken. Through words we have access to the ideas of our ancestors if we are willing to trace back the meanings of our words as far as we can trace them. By doing so, we have an opportunity to reinvigorate Truth as it was known by our ancestors, who I like to affectionately refer to as our Greatest Grandparents (our GGs).

TRUTH'S PREREQUISITE
The prerequisite to seeing Truth accurately, is to develop the ability to "perceive correctly," which depends on knowing how to look. Fortunately, our GGs left specific instructions in the living word of Patañjali's Yoga Sūtras for correct perception, which will be introduced in this book. We'll also be applying those same principles of correct perception throughout so that we may accurately and irrefutably identify the Truth about the Fountain of Youth.

TRUTH'S COREQUISITE
Here's a cool and quick little exercise: Grab a pencil and piece of paper. Write the word OBLIVIOUS in all caps. Then, erase the third and fourth letters L and I. What are you left with? This exercise demonstrates what happens when we remove the lie, the removal of lies being Truth's corequisite. We've been clouded with many lies, so much that it's virtually impossible for us to see what's obvious and True, even when it's right in front of us, without really putting forth the effort to see what's obvious and True. A major

reason why when we hear the words "the fountain of youth is in you and I" they don't register at first, is because of all the lies we unconsciously accept as true. The PRIMARY GOAL of this book is to make the Fountain of Youth utterly obvious, so you may know its Truth. In order to do so, many lies must be removed, and this book is dedicated to that end. One lie, among many we'll dispose of, is that Yoga and The Bible are incompatible. Nothing could be further from the Truth. And, as it happens, unbeknownst to practically everyone (regular churchgoers and Bible bashers alike), one of the major themes of the Bible is The Fountain of Youth, as you will begin to see from reading this book, AND yoga has everything to do with it.

(KJV) JOHN 1:1
In the beginning was the word, and the word was with God, and the word was God.

WORDS ARE POLLEN PRESERVING TRUTH
When we consider the regions where Spanish, English, French, Italian, and the gamut of supposed Proto-Indo European (PIE) languages developed (which includes Greek, and Sanskrit according to modern linguists), as well as Hebrew, Ethiopic, Arabic, and ALL LANGUAGES OF OUR PLANET outside of PIE, we must also consider the tendency of language to cross-pollinate. An important point to know or remember is that the spoken tongues of people were never contained in neat little boxes with strict linguistic rules and undeviating dialects, like schools and scholars may seem to argue, suggest, portray, and propagate today. People traveled and took their dialects and colloquialisms with them wherever they went, as we do now, and the spoken words of varying regions have always influenced the spoken words of other regions by these factors and forces — language is fluid. As a result, the ways certain words and their associated sounds were pronounced would have had lots of variances, due to the influences of people's birth tongues and native languages and would have been understood by and effectively communicated to others from different villages and regions, despite colorful expressions, slight differences in syntax, and/or how words were pronounced. We can go to different areas spread throughout English speaking countries and find these same differences yet be able to communicate perfectly with people. At

the same time, when we visit places, we pick up sayings that we take with us to other places we travel. It's as if we are butterflies, bees, and hummingbirds, and words are pollen.

In 1000, 2000, or 5000 years from now, it's doubtful that linguists, anthropologists, and/or historians of the day will have the slightest clue about where the following phrases, statements, and expressions come from, what they mean, or how they originated: MJ is the GOAT; I'm a couch potato who likes to pig out while watching my favorite sitcoms; Gittin' jiggy wit it; and, That fit is on fleek af. Let's just analyze and speculate on the first one, MJ is the GOAT. Might some future researcher surmise that an MJ must be some type of ruminant related to sheep and goats that must also be extinct since they've never seen an MJ in their lifetime? Why not (?), it's definitely logical. To us this might seem ridiculous because we know that MJ represents the initials of someone's name who is famous, like Michael Jackson or Michael Jordan, since GOAT means Greatest Of All Time. Even in our time, though, not everyone would agree, because MJ as the GOAT might also be Magic Johnson, Mahalia Jackson, Mick Jagger, or Mary Jane, depending on who you ask.

The arguments of future researchers might sound logical, plausible, and convincing to the people of their time, yet be far off the mark of Truth. At best, they'd be making the wildest of guesses. Heck, many of us today might not be clear on what some of these words and expressions mean and from where they originate. The point is, if future researchers would be guessing about us, and in all probability be DEAD WRONG about the origins and meanings of these phrases, why should we expect any different or better from today's researchers (who feel no kindred ancestral connection) about what they have to say about OUR GGs and what our GGs were saying? It's imperative that we think for ourselves. We can do our own best guessing. At least we feel a kindred connection to our ancestors, and by asking, seeking, and knocking with a genuine desire to KNOW THYSELF, we are more likely to connect the right dots of INNER-STANDing and be inspired toward the best for ALL, the Most High.

"When I let go of who I am, I become what I might be." ~Lau Tzu

EXCITING TIMES

A new age is upon us, where we are no longer obliged to keep closed minds tethered to traditions of noncontemplative routines reliant on thoughtlessness, blind faith and conviction, while, without investigation or resistance, uncritically trusting doctrines imposed by governmental institutions whose primary objective has always been to promote, establish, and assert its own control. Knowledge and wisdom, like cool, refreshing, pure water on a sweltering summer day, can, if it's to retain its purity, only be poured into a cup that's open, clean, and empty (not absent) — and the cup is the mind. We must learn to let go of who we have been, so that we may become what we are meant to be, just as the caterpillar.

Truth, on the other hand, is the oasis sought by knowledge and wisdom. Any time Truth can be found and sipped upon, a deep thirst is quenched. A huge mistake many of us make when it comes to finding Truth, is that we spend most of our time, if not all, looking for truth (with a lower case t) rather than polishing the lens through which we look to find Truth. The mind is the lens of perception and can only perceive as well as it is round and free of film and blemish.

This book strives to reveal the Truth about the fountain of youth and what yoga has to do with it while applying the principles of correct perception and its criteria as put forth by our GGs in the profound and practical philosophy of Patañjali's Yoga Sūtras. By practicing what the sūtras preach, the aim is to maintain the integrity of the message contained therein and to accurately discern what's real from what is not. When we know how to adhere to the criteria of correct perception, and how to apply them, then we are no longer dependent on other researchers and authors to do the thinking for us, because we will know how to confidently think competently for ourselves. Toward the beginning of our discussion, we'll look at what Patañjali's Yoga Sūtras say about the mind and the prerequisites necessary to exercise correct perception and NOT be perpetual victims of our own distortions.

Damon Givehand

Part 1

REMOVING LIES & INSPIRING CHURCH

(KJV) MATTHEW 10:16
Behold, I send you forth as sheep in the midst of wolves: be ye therefore wise as serpents, and harmless as doves.

Damon Givehand

♦ IT'S REAL ♦

There is a FOUNTAIN OF YOUTH and IT IS REAL. We've always heard of this spring of water that reverses aging and restores youth to anyone who drinks of it or bathes in it, even allowing them to live forever, as if it were a myth; AND, we've always been led to believe it's OUT THERE somewhere. If Ponce De Leon ever was in search of this place, believed by him to be located somewhere in what is now recognized as the geographic state of Florida on the North American continent, at least according to the "story" we're told, he was never ever near the Truth in any of his supposed excursions. It's not out there — any such stories are fruitless fairy tales — it's within. And NOT within in the metaphysical sense, although that too, but THE FOUNTAIN is a real and tangible part of our physical bodies. By the end of this book you'll know WHAT the fountain of youth is, and WHERE it is, among many other things you'll be exposed to in order to SEE RIGHT.

"All Truth passes through 3 stages: FIRST it's ridiculed; SECOND, it's violently opposed; and THIRD, it's accepted as self-evident." ~ commonly attributed to Arthur Schopenhauer

♦ TRUTH AS IS, NOT AS WISHED ♦

If it's complicated, it's not rooted in TRUTH. Truth is NEVER complicated! While Truth isn't complicated, it is tricky because it relies on people's ability to see correctly in a material society that often profits to the degree that people don't see correctly. People's ignorance is and has been commonly exploited, and there is and has even been incentive to foster, promote, and facilitate ignorance amongst the masses, making it easy for a relative few to capitalize, while building financial fortunes and acquiring governmental, institutional, and corporate control. The relative few who hold positions of power over the people, even stir up confusion and exert the power they wield at the expense of people's health and wellbeing, so they can live luxurious lives while not having to work at all, despite it ultimately being to their own detriment (unbeknownst to them). This is nothing new, but rather an age-old problem.

This problem of perception (seeing correctly or incorrectly) is so old and so serious, that our GGs dealt with it long ago, and we are blessed that the solutions they discovered, developed, and perfected have been preserved enough that we may put the pieces back together today. The body of work known as the Yoga Sūtras that were organized in the name of Patañjali represents an effective response to the problem, because it involves correcting the mind — our instrument of perception (or seeing).

> "If you CORRECT your mind, the rest of your life will fall into place." ~ Lao Tzu (6th century BCE)

Patañjali's Yoga Sūtras identify five "activities of the mind" in sūtra 1.6, and they are (as given in their transliterated Sanskrit) pramāna, viparyaya, vikalpa, nidrā, and smṛti, which are loosely translated as right perception, misperception, imagination, dreamless sleep, and memory, respectively. The very next sūtra (1.7) then goes on to list three criteria for right perception as 1) direct sensory input (pratyaksha), 2) competent inference (anumāna), and 3) reliable and trustworthy reference or testimony (āgamāha).

What's important to note in Patañjali's Yoga Sūtras is that everything is given in a deliberate and intentional order. Correct perception is listed as first of the five activities of mind, because of its foremost importance. This is not to suggest that the other activities of mind are not important, because they are all invaluable. Likewise, when the criteria for right perception are given, they're given in a specific order for a reason. Patañjali gives the criteria for correct perception (or right knowledge) in order of weight and rank regarding their authenticity, validity, reliability, and accuracy, which means our direct sensory input (i.e. first-hand perception based on actual experience and exposure or "being there") is what we should rely on FIRST for CORRECT PERCEPTION (or right knowledge). Pratyaksha literally means "in front of eyes" (3rd eye included). By building our knowledge starting with what our senses pick up directly, and what we experience and witness first-hand, we will be able to, with the right effort, make inferences based on sound reasoning (connecting the right dots), which will also endow us with the discernment to know what third-party sources represent valid and trustworthy testimony (especially during unusually corrupt times like we live in now), as we work to correct our instrument of perception and answer our own unique QUESTIONS.

While ALL the activities of mind are invaluable and a natural part of our makeup, PERCEPTION is the key to pain, pleasure, servitude, or salvation. Unfortunately, the commercial world we live in is replete with misinformation, primarily because the profits to be made by business organizations hinge on consumer emotion and behavior. As a result, lots of money is spent on influencing societal beliefs in order to convert people into life-long consumers and loyal customers, so as to favorably impact companies' bottom lines by any means necessary. Some readers might think it extreme to use language like "by any means necessary" when referring to profit-driven corporate organizations, but the truth of this fact can be observed when looking into parent companies who simultaneously own processed food and artificial sweetener companies alongside sister companies that manufacture pharmaceutical products claiming to remedy the maladies caused by consuming processed food and synthetic sweeteners — a clear CONFLICT OF INTEREST.

The point of the foregoing paragraph is to put all individuals interested in living the highest quality life possible ON NOTICE about the importance of correct perception. Once you find out the Truth about the fountain of youth, you will see why I invest as much time as I do up front laying a proper foundation. The Truth is hard enough to see on its own, given our natural human inclinations and tendencies to simply accept what we assume without thinking — misinformation and disinformation only compound the challenge.

Following are a few of the common BIG mistakes people make, although there are many more, that preclude them from coming to know the Truth regarding the subject matter of this book, and when they're confronted with these mistakes, they just as commonly resist acknowledging and admitting them due to a lifetime of indoctrination and an unwillingness to be totally honest with themselves (the price that must be paid by any and all looking to enter the gates of Truth). Learning the Truth forces people to be accountable for and to themselves, a responsibility most would rather do without.

♦ 3 MAJOR MODERN MISTAKES ♦

Three major modern mistakes obscuring big picture truth are…

MISTAKE #1
ASSUMING WE HUMANS ARE NOT ALL KIN

Let us begin by first establishing that all human beings are of one creation and we are one family. We might be a ridiculously dysfunctional family at the moment, because our intelligence has been undermined and corrupted by education, innuendo, and media propaganda, but WE ARE FAMILY. We must stop adopting divisive ideologies that cause us to see ourselves as separate from one another and begin again to embrace our familial likeness and affinity. Some of the main isms and ideas driving concepts of division among the human family today are those of race, nationality, gender, politics, economic status, sexual preference, religion, and savage, animalistic dogmas like survival of the fittest versus survival of the village. We must remember that a divided people are a conquered people.

It's time we work at becoming a cohesive and harmonious family unit once again, and the place to begin is in correcting our own minds — not correcting other people's minds but correcting our own. No one can correct anyone else's mind. The only one who can correct a person's mind is the person. EVERYONE'S mind is in need of correcting, whether the person recognizes and acknowledges it or not, and this is simply a natural consequence of having been born into the world, the nature of the mind and how we learn, and being told what to think rather than being taught how to think and see, while developing tendencies, triggered reactions, and habit patterns based on misperceptions we're groomed to assume represent reality. It's time to un-divide ourselves and become unconquered.

MISTAKE #2
THINKING WE ARE NOT THE GREATEST GRAND CHILDREN OF THE ANCIENTS, AND THAT THEY WERE NOT A CULTURED, CULTIVATED, AND HIGHLY SOPHISTICATED PEOPLE (ALL TRAITS WE'VE INHERITED)

Not only have we been divided from each other, we've been divided from ourselves, and from our forefathers and mothers. Think of the love of a parent to child, grandparent to grandchild, great grandparent to great grandchild, great great grandparent to great great grandchild. With the extension of each living generation, the love only gets wiser, stronger, and more tender. We are the children of our parents. We are the grandchildren of our parent's parents. We are the great grandchildren of our parent's parents' parents. We are the great great grandchildren of our parent's parents' parents' parents. And so on... We are the Great Offspring of our ancestor GGs who lived many millennia before us. We are a collage and culmination of all our collective parents back through time, and capable of all they ever accomplished. We are ONE TREE. We are them.

And, not only did our GGs develop pyramid technology that continues to boggle the minds of popular scientists today, our GGs also developed a science for perfecting the most amazing, awe-inspiring, technological instrument ever conceived — the HUMAN BRAIN, BODY, MIND, and SPIRIT. The Yoga Sūtras of Patañjali are an ancient guidebook on how to correct our minds by purifying the brain, body, and soul so that our spirits may flower as intended. In the first seven sūtras of chapter 1 of Patañjali's Yoga Sūtras (called Samādhi Pāda), we are told WHAT yoga is, what tends to happen when we are NOT in a state of yoga, the five activities of the mind and their consequences, as well as the criteria for CORRECT PERCEPTION, among other supremely relevant and vital things. Clearly, Patañjali's Yoga Sūtras are not the work of an unadvanced, non-thinking people unconcerned with the quality of human existence. The ancients (who we are an extension of) were utterly concerned with the quality and condition of the human being, and the same blood that flowed through them flows through us!

The field of modern psychology, on the other hand, has yet to unravel the mysteries of correct perception and how to develop the mental acuity and keenness to discern Truth from ILLusion, allowing the human being to ascend back to man's destined divine status. And this should not come as too much of a surprise since this field of study is in its infancy, being less than 150 years old at the time of this writing, which is barely (if even) an embryo compared to that of the ancients, which is "at least" tens of thousands of years old (but probably a lot older than that). The immaturity of this field of study, and its extreme un-development, is reflected in its attitude as a discipline.

By placing so much concern over the "study of human behavior" and so much interest in developing methods for controlling human behavior and methods of motivation that ultimately serve corporations (no wonder "government" reveres this field so), government education makes its underhanded intentions obvious. Psychology actually doesn't mean "the study of human behavior," but rather "the study of the soul/spirit" (where we have psyche "soul or animating spirit" + -logy "study of") which was a primary interest of our GGs. Controlling human behavior as it relates to whole societies is a CHILDISH pursuit in terms of the age and level of development of civilizations. Patañjali's Yoga Sūtras have to do with the control of human behavior too, but with the control of the person over her or his own behavior by way of working with their own mind and body (not other people's).

It's the modern lack of knowledge pertaining to the mind and well-being (not to mention Love) that causes fellow humans to war with each other and remain perpetually in external and internal conflict. This lack of knowledge is also the reason healthcare (a misnomer, which might more accurately be referred to as "dis-ease management") is such a profitable industry/market. Good thing we have access to records left to us from the past by our ancient GGs, the ones whose love was and is the wisest, strongest, and most tender of all.

MISTAKE #3
TRUSTING THE UNTRUSTWORTHY EVEN BEFORE WE TRUST OUR OWN SENSES

The ancients were NOT primitive people incapable of advanced thinking, as we are led to unconsciously accept and assume by the story education attempts to indoctrinate us into believing about the past. It is conceivable, on the other hand, that our current education system would teach that our ancestors were primitive, unadvanced thinkers, since, as most of us have probably heard and can easily fathom, that history ("his story") is written by the victors (not to mention that our ancestor GGs were focused on LIBERATION and FREEDOM while today's corporate governments focus on REGULATIONS, PERMITS, and PROFIT — which is nothing more than external CONTROL, for a fee incurred by the person being controlled on top of that).

The primary objective of government is to manage populations, and by projecting and asserting itself as the ruling entity, has grown incredibly effective at accomplishing exactly what the word government suggests — govern "to control" + ment (from Latin mentalis) "of the mind." Big government is nothing more than an instrument used to control the minds of those who agree to fall UNDER its leadership or rulership, and why a primary objective of education is so focused on its students UNDER-STANDing versus OVER-STANDing or INNER-STANDing (even when some people hear the expression "overstand" they react like "what the heck is that?").

Without knowledge of Self, people are ill-equipped to govern themselves, and modern-day compulsion schooling teaches doctrine that erodes perception (in general and of Self) rather than facilitates the learning of Self. When people don't know who they truly are, they are less able to govern themselves from the inside and are more likely to agree with being governed from the outside to keep them from harming themselves or each other. This way of thinking, perceiving, and seeing things (by the people), is necessary for the control and management of a subservient society willing to voluntarily forfeit their sovereignty (a term most are oblivious to or whose meaning they are completely ignorant of due to the education they received) in exchange for "protection" — protection they've been educated and led to believe they need.

Governments (different than governance), especially unjust, oppressive, and divisive types, can quell the potential and possibility of being overthrown if they can effectively control the beliefs of its citizens. Therefore, based on the inherent motives of a government (not sentimentally connected with its subjects) to be in control and to amass more power, and recognizing no kinship or kindred connection (which can be observed by looking at the conditions of the people), the story told to students by government education, especially public education, is always suspect of being spun to shape the minds of the rank and file who matriculate through the sophisticated machinery of education we openly call "institutions," in order to cultivate a servile, obedient, and predictable society most unlikely of upheaval. It doesn't matter what race a person proclaims, gender, religious proclivities, or anything of the sort; just look at all the people who are addicted to drugs (prescription or otherwise); all the people who are struggling with health (cancer, depression, anxiety, obesity, diabetes, or any autoimmune disease, etc.); all the people who are essentially debt slaves (who live to pay the monthly bills, can't afford to take the vacation they really want, and who look forward to the weekends while dreading Mondays); and all those who are more concerned with their credit scores than the well-being of their neighbors. All these people come from all races, sexes, nationalities, genders, religions, sexual preferences, political parties, economic classes, etc. The maladies and troubles of today are a reflection of the leadership that led us here, exposing their UNTRUSTWORTHINESS.

Some of us are fortunate to have a fire in us that is impossible to extinguish, no matter if UNTRUSTWORTHY FORCES try to snuff it out or what strategies are put in motion to smother it. Yet, for many others, arguably the vast majority, the intricate and sophisticated system of schooling has been wildly successful at educating out of them, any inspiration or desire to thrive, while replacing it with tolerance and a tired and feeble, hopeless hope. Knowledge of the real and actual Fountain of Youth can get us back on track to Truly Live again, because WE WILL LIVE

AGAIN (it's not a matter of "if" we will, but rather "when" we will). The time has come! The time is NOW!!!

♦ WHAT GOES AROUND COMES BACK AROUND ♦

The cycle of time is reliable and trustworthy. As we all can observe in the short term, time is cyclic. We can see the cycle of time as we go from day to night to day again; and we can see the cycle of time as we go from one year to the next, each year passing through the same successive seasons. Our GGs spoke of larger cycles of time, and they spoke of four distinct ages which are woven into the grandest cycle of all, the Great Year, the four ages being: 1) the Golden Age, 2) the Silver Age, 3) the Bronze Age, and 4) the Iron Age. Even the French word siècle, which is commonly understood as "century," literally means "an age," and sprinkles on a little more evidence that time cycles through ages. Listen, and you can hear "cycle" when you say siècle — it's in the sound. And, remember that the spoken word can and often does preserve Truth for generations to come.

The Great Year, also known as the precession of the equinoxes, is approximately 24,000 years (25,800 or 26,000 according to some sources), or 2400 siècles, and not obvious to us as individuals, because we simply do not live long enough to directly observe the cycle(s) for ourselves, like we can with a day, a month, and a year. Even if we lived for 200 years, we would only see 200 years of a 24,000 year cycle, which calculates to less than 1% of a circle (less than one second on a clock). So it's easy to grasp how such a large cycle of time could go utterly unnoticed by discordant societies consumed with competing, surviving (as opposed to thriving), and winning ON THE GROUND, and be completely unconsidered by individuals.

Yet, somehow our GGs lived in such uninterrupted harmony for so long, that they were able to pass along trustworthy knowledge and information from one generation to the next until they eventually observed that humanity cycles through these ages. This means they would have had to observe this phenomenon for multiple 24,000-year cycles in order to identify and establish a pattern, and then study the effects of the pattern on human behavior/experience, giving us authentic astrology and the zodiacal sciences. How many hundreds of thousands of years do you suspect they (really we, since they are our greatest grandparents and we are their distant grandchildren/offspring) had to go through in order to gather, store, and study this knowledge? History is written by the victors… no wonder we're not taught this in school.

♦ LIGHT IN A DARK AGE ♦

Patañjali's Yoga Sūtras come to us from a Golden Age, a time when the individual and collective consciousness of humans and humanity was at a peak. As we cycled out of a Golden era and descended through Silver and Bronze ages, human consciousness declined until we bottomed out in the pit of an Iron Age, aka Dark Age, which we are currently beginning to cycle out of now. Many involved in the "real" science of astrology say we are now at the beginning of transitioning from a Piscean Age to an Aquarian Age, or from an age of belief to an age of knowing.

Belief is the absence of knowledge, just as darkness is the absence of light. Sight is the ability for open eyes to see when light is present, and this may take place in the physical outside world OR in our minds. A key characteristic of a "dark" age is that the light required for open eyes to see is severely diminished or entirely blocked (and therefore absent). In our minds, we call sight (or the eye's ability to see) knowledge and wisdom, and because this knowledge is in the inside world (our minds), we call this IN-SIGHT. When light is absent or does not shine inside, we call that kind of darkness IGNORANCE — a state of mind whereby we ignore things without knowing we're ignoring them simply because we cannot see them in the dark.

Notice the root word IGNORE in IGNORANCE. In an IRON AGE (aka Dark Age), like we are on the cusp of coming out of now, the masses by and large IGNORE certain obvious truths in favor of ideas and beliefs they've been taught to accept as true, despite the ease with which these beliefs can be proved false. For instance, anyone can heal themselves of dis-ease through cleansing (detoxing), moving the body, proper breathing, getting ample rest, soaking up plenty of direct sunlight, holding pleasant and joyous thoughts, and maintaining a harmonious and positively constructive attitude; but most people don't "believe" so, let alone know so, because of false beliefs that have been cleverly planted in their minds by education and media propaganda. Some people will even read the previous sentence and argue against it, basing all the elements of their argument on some idea(s) they've been convinced of through indoctrination, which means they are loaded with BELIEF (aka "not knowing").

Most people have been educated, trained, and conditioned to be morally and intellectually lazy, so they favor BELIEFS (that they've been fed and now find comfort in, like comfort food) and superficial opinions over actually applying any effort to do and practice what must be done in order to SEE CORRECTLY AND KNOW FOR THEMSELVES. Knowing requires too much work for a lot of people.

To drive the point home, continuing with our "dis-ease" example from above, consider that instead of people doing and practicing certain things to find out if its possible to heal themselves, they mindlessly follow the advice of their medically "educated" and "trained" doctors. These doctors, while usually well-meaning and not inherently evil people, just thoroughly indoctrinated from all the years of intense and rigorous "advanced" schooling, often offer the advice to undergo some invasive and irreversible operation and/or to take some toxic prescription drugs. And when patients take the drugs prescribed to them by their doctors, those drugs come with their own long list of possible "side effects" (a euphemism) that, if the patient suffers from any, will in turn require even more drugs to remedy, which come with yet their own slew of side-effects, and so on. Even the expression side effects reveals how we've been manipulated through language into "seeing" in a way that benefits profit-driven companies by making what are actually the "effects" of drugs seem trivial, by calling them "side" effects. Most of today's health complications are the EFFECTS of polluted blood, clogged bowels, and toxified livers, not "side" effects, plain and simple. Truth is not complicated.

Government (whether corporate, institutional, or otherwise) promoted ignorance is a darkness loaded with sinister motive; and its objective has always been to distract humans from their innate power, a feat they've been incredibly successful at for at least the past couple thousand years, so long that we've been generally lulled into thinking this is just the way it is and the way it shall remain. The evidence of its success can be seen in people's willingness to accept what schools teach AND what the media projects as truth, without any investigation or resistance, even though this propagated education strips individuals mentally of their independent power and sovereignty. This is what has happened, a remarkable achievement of government. It's time for everyday people to once again take control of their own minds, and take care of their health, which directly relates to the REAL Fountain of Youth.

Fortunately, we live during a time when people are figuring out that blind belief in government sanctioned ideas not only does not serve the people, but instead it undermines people's wellbeing entirely in practically every way (physically, mentally, emotionally, intellectually, spiritually, etc.). Although, during dark iron ages, the gullibility of the vast majority is prevalent, there have always been small pockets of people serving as exceptions to the majority rule of ignorance, otherwise YOU would not be reading this. YOU represent members of those small pockets of people that are the exception to the rule. As a side note, isn't it interesting that the expression Iron Age contains in it the letters I-G-N-O-R-E, and the Latin root of ignore, which is ignorare, contains the letters I-R-O-N-A-G-E? I'm just putting it out there.

♦ THE TRUSTWORTHIEST ♦

The advice we get from our ancestor GGs is to exercise the principles of correct perception, which again, in order of verity, integrity, and importance are: direct sensory input, competent inference, and reliable, trustworthy reference. This wisdom is passed on to us so that we may eventually figure out how to cultivate a mind at ease. The advice and encouragement we get from the current government is to go to school and get good grades, get a good job, buy a home, pay our bills, and leave the real thinking up to who "they" approve and "deem" qualified, because science is too complicated and difficult for the rank and file to comprehend. These two scenarios make it clear who encourages the people to ignore AND who encourages people to trust their own senses and cognitive abilities. Who does your gut and heart tell you is more trustworthy?

♦ HAVE CHURCH & GET PREGNANT POR FAVOR ♦

(KJV) LUKE 17:20-21
(20) And when he was demanded of the Pharisees, when the kingdom of God should come, he answered them and said, The kingdom of God cometh not with observation: (21) Neither shall they say, Lo here! or, lo there! for, behold, the kingdom of God is within you.

Church has become something entirely different than what it was born as and what it's intended to stand for, as is shown through some etymological investigative work. A quick search into the origins of the word church reveals, at its root, the Greek word kyrios (sometimes spelled kurios, although less and less commonly these days), meaning "ruler, master, lord," and the PIE word keue "to swell, swollen" (keue being the "ky" pronunciation in kyrios — remember this when we discuss the Spanish word pregunta meaning "question"). Further, kyrios and curious are homonyms, meaning they are pronounced exactly the same. Curious means "eager to know, inquisitive" and inquisitive means "making inquiry" and "asking questions." According to Strong's Concordance (an exhaustive index of every word in the King James Version Bible), Kyrios is also a title used to refer to God (remember this when we get to the section discussing the diencephalon in the brain).

So, church has to do with being curious, as can be seen by its phonetic Greek twin kyrios. How the Greeks understood kyrios, in terms of church, indicates how we should treat our curiosity. By allowing our curiosity (i.e. questions) to rule us and serve as our master or lord, we are led on a QUEST (meaning "to seek" and is the root of the word question,) to find remedy for ALL that ails us. This is what (KJV) Matthew 7:7-12 is talking about when it says to ASK, SEEK, and KNOCK. The cure, "cure" meaning to "heal, make whole" and being the root of the word curious, is what our questions truly SEEK, which is a search for what can heal us and make us whole (i.e. holy/wholly). It's that part of us that's inquisitive and eager to know (Truth) that is to rule and guide us as our Master. Nowhere in the origin of the word church is "a building" ever mentioned. (KJV) Luke 17:21 lets us know that "...the kingdom of God is within you." Church is not someplace we go, it's something we have! So HAVE CHURCH!

The word for "to ask a question" in Spanish is pregunta, which is strikingly similar to the English word pregnant, as they share the root preg. There are some "smart people" in the world with a lot of education who argue there is no linguistic relationship between pregnant and pregunta, and there are some smart ones who argue there is a relationship. Just because some haven't been able to figure out the relationship, doesn't make it necessarily true that one does not exist. Remember, they're guessing, and they're often people who tend to only regurgitate what they recall being taught (really told) and trained to accept as "correct answers" in their respective educational programs (and anyone "programmed" has been "trained to behave in a predetermined way" which is predictable). These people, whose arguments are based solely and strictly on what they were told to think in school, not thinking for themselves, trust the mysterious stewards of their government education before they trust their own senses and ability to connect the dots for themselves (and this is a violation of Patañjali's criteria for correct perception).

Applying the principle of direct sensory input and competent inference (both generally superior to reference), we can see and hear the similarity of pregnant and pregunta in spelling and pronunciation; but these by themselves, are not enough to conclude anything, these are just observations to note (direct sensory input). If we happen to take into account the PIE words keue and prek, however, the evidence of a connection shared with pregunta and pregnant begins to become more evident.

Again, keue (the root of kyrios and the first syllable pronunciation of the ky in kyrios) means "to swell, swollen" just like what can be observed in a pregnant belly; and prek means "ask, to make inquiry, to question" as also suggested by the homonym curious and the Spanish word pregunta. If these words, pregunta and pregnant, were spelled with a k instead of a g, giving us prek-unta and preknant, then the connection shared between these words might be more obvious. And, as it happens, this could have been the case on record, since k and g are gutturals over which linguists charged with "re-constructing" PIE have argued (in the centrum versus satem debate). Let's face it, THEY JUST DON'T KNOW which is why there's an argument in the first place. They are just as clueless as linguists a thousand years from now would be about the origin and meaning of MJ is the GOAT. Why should we leave it up to them to decide without investing any of our own thought? Who's doing this "re-constructing" anyway? And why should we blindly trust that "they" are trustworthy? (On behalf of whose interests do they work?)

When we let our curious questions (preguntas) guide and rule us, we become pregnant with something that swells in the BELLies of our brains (cereBELLums) that we'll one day give birth to, or manifest, as a result of our unique personal quest (asking, seeking, and knocking to find answers to our own deep questions — to ASK, SEEK, and KNOCK... hmmm... where do we think the expression "KNOCKed up" comes from?). This pregnancy is more than figurative, but more on this later when we get into revealing the REAL Fountain of Youth.

What's the big deal with establishing whether or not pregnant and pregunta are connected anyway? Because it reveals the value of being curious and inquisitive, while spotlighting the unknown meaning of church, and that this pregnancy, coming from an eagerness to know how to cure our Life leads to being born again into everlasting life (notice even that the words KNOw and KNOck share the root kno which is also gno, as in gnosis).

The Flood talked about in the Bible (involving NOah and The Ark) has to do with when the water of this pregnancy breaks (more on this later as well). That said, DO NOT LET THIS WORLD ABORT YOUR PREK-NANCY OR KILL YOUR CURE-IOSITY TO ASK, SEEK, AND KNOCK!!! To do so would be like aborting all your yet unborn seeds of genius (see and hear "gene" in genius?) that, if allowed to be conceived, brooded, and hatched (asking, seeking, and knocking), will surely lead to a life of the highest quality and ultimate freedom at the very least (and at the most, experience Heaven on Earth, which is when millions of currently dormant brain cells activate causing an experience of life through 360 senses versus the 5 or 6 we are taught about in today's schools — more on this in a forthcoming book, but in the meantime you are encouraged to read GODMAN: The Word Made Flesh by George Washington Carey, 1845-1924).

♦ A WHISPER FROM THE PAST ♦

(KJV) MATTHEW 7:7-8
(7) ASK, and it shall be given you; SEEK, and ye shall find; KNOCK, and it shall be OPENed unto you: (8) For every one that asketh receiveth; and he that seeketh findeth; and to him that knocketh it shall be opened.

To ASK, SEEK, and KNOCK are not words to be taken or uttered lightly. In our modern world we've been lulled and encouraged to sleep on the power and true meanings of these terms. Other than being equivalent to the PIE word prek, ASK means "demand" (from Old Saxon escon). To SEEK (from Old English secan) means "inquire, pursue" and (PIE sag) "track down." To KNOCK (from Old English cnocian) means "pound, beat." So you see, these terms carry with them a spirit of active vigor, not passive and casual lackadaisicalness. To ASK, SEEK, and KNOCK is serious business! If we truly wish to know the Truth about the Fountain of Youth, then we must ASK, SEEK, and KNOCK; or, in other words, we must DEMAND to know the Truth, PURSUE and TRACK DOWN the Truth, and POUND on the door of Truth until it's answered and opened or until the doors are BEATen DOWN.

♦ THE BIBLE & THE FOUNTAIN ♦

Among other things, the Bible is a book about The Fountain. The word bible and the Spanish word biblioteca ("library") share the Latin verb root bibō (whose present infinitive is bibere) which means "drink" and shows up in the Old French word imbiber (embiber) "to soak in," as well as the Latin imbibere "drink in, inhale, absorb." Just listen to how closely bible and bibō sound when you say them out loud — they sound almost identical (depending on whether you pronounce the L in bible or not). Further, the word library is connected to libation, meaning "a pouring out of wine in honor of God, or a god" or simply "a drink offering." The Greek word leibein, meaning "to pour or make libation," has as its root the PIE term lei- meaning "to flow, pour out, drip." The expression for "purified water" in the Bible is nothing more than Virgin Mary, where virgin means "purified" and Mary means "water" (which can be seen in the words MARIne and MARItime, both meaning "of the sea, pertaining to the sea" where Latin mare simply means "sea"— again, more on this later). Keep all this in mind as we explore the REAL Fountain of Youth.

♦ THE BIBLE & YOGA FIT LIKE HAND-IN-GLOVE ♦

The Bible and Yoga are a match made in Heaven, which becomes obvious when applying the principles of "correct perception" as described in Patañjali's Yoga Sūtras, YS 1.7 specifically. LOOKING with eyes that can see and LISTENING with ears that can hear, let's begin with our direct senses to witness firsthand how the Bible and Yoga fit so perfectly together.

First, consider the meaning of the word Yoga. Merriam-Webster gives the (Sanskrit) origin as literally "yoking" from yunakti "he yokes" akin to Latin jungere "to join". It's also worth mentioning that the Sanskrit and PIE roots of yoga are yuj and yeug- (homonyms), respectively, meaning "to yoke, join, unite." And when we look into how Merriam-Webster describes the meaning of yoke (n.), we find its first definition given as "a wooden bar or frame by which TWO draft animals, typically OXEN, are joined at the heads or necks for working together." Additionally, dictionary.com offers these two definitions: 1) a device for joining together a PAIR of draft animals, especially OXEN, usually consisting of a crosspiece with two bow-shaped pieces, each enclosing the head of an animal; AND 2), a pair of draft animals fastened together by a yoke. You can pick any dictionary you want and find the same definitions referring to TWO DRAFT ANIMALS (OR A PAIR), PRIMARILY OXEN. These definitions are deliberate with their emphasis on TWO OXEN, not "a few" and not "several" but TWO, A PAIR(!); and not any animal but typically OXEN. Look to see with your own eyes — direct sensory input!

Now, it's important that we LISTEN to the sound produced when we say words, and not get confused by spellings. Say the word BIBLE out loud so you can hear for yourself with your own ears (direct sensory input). Now repeat it, but this time say it slowly emphasizing each syllable one at a time. What do you hear when you say BI-BLE? You hear BI + BULL. The prefix "BI" means "two." Two what? Two BULLS. OXEN are bulls, or DRAFT ANIMALS, although oxen are very special kinds of bulls (because they've been castrated — having to do with brahmacharya, one of the yamas in aṣṭaṅga yoga, and Heaving Nun which I'll cover in a forthcoming book; but again you are encouraged to pick up a copy of GODMAN: The Word Made Flesh by George Washington Carey and see the section called THE RIB-LAH THAT MADE THE WOM(B)MAN on pg 95 where he talks about Heaven being "heave nun"). Hearing the actual sound pronounced with our own ears when we say the name of the Good Book is working directly with our sensory input. At this point you might be thinking, "Yea, that's clever and all, but it's only coincidence and doesn't mean anything." Ok, let's go a step further.

A key verse in the KJV Bible (Matthew 13:34) reads "All these things spake Jesus unto the multitude in parables; and without a parable spake he not unto them." EVERYTHING spoken by Jesus in the Bible (BI-BULL) is written in parables. Do you hear it? Say "parables" out loud, slowly emphasizing each syllable one at a time. Ahhh... you get PAIR + 'A (of) + BULLS. On top of that, the 5 books of Moses in the Old Testament, the Pentateuch, is called the Torah, which is pronounced like Taurus, the BULL of the Zodiac, minus the ending "s" (in Taurus). LISTEN with ears prepared to hear and don't get thrown off by spellings. [Spellings are just spells cast to confuse, taught in grammar schools (the word grammar being etymologically linked to "magic" by way of Old French gramare, gramaire) where we were also taught to write in cursive ("curse" + "ive"). Hmmm... what's really going on here?]

Further, any good yoga teacher will let you know that YOGA is about STEERing all the faculties/activities of your mind in ONE DIRECTION, yoking them, so as to give your FULL ATTENTION TO. Another interesting and undeniable fact is that the word STEER in noun form means "young ox, bullock, bull" and is further defined as "a male bovine that is castrated before sexual maturity" just like oxen, by definition, are castrated (castration which again gets into brahmacharya in the aṣṭaṅga — see Patañjali's Yoga Sūtras 2.30 and 2.38 — and having to do with what it means to "heave nun").

So yoga means yoke, and a yoke is a cross-piece joining TWO OXEN or a "pair of bulls" at the neck. Phonetically, "Bible" is pronounced BI + BULL, and Jesus, the main character of the Good Book, spoke only in parables, which pronounced out loud sounds like PAIR 'O BULLS ("pair of bulls"). This is an UNDENIABLE, OBVIOUS, and uncomplicated connection shared by Yoga and the Bible that you can see with your own eyes and hear with your own ears, without having to take anyone's word for it on blind faith.

It may not be obvious at this point that these Bulls have to do with The Fountain of Youth, but by the end of this book it should be made obvious. Before we go there though, let's look at some other breadcrumbs (aside from the spoken word) our GGs left to direct our attention toward the glorious Fountain of Youth, and where it's located.

♦ BREADCRUMBS FROM OUR GGs ♦

Our GG's have been trying to tell us where to look all along, although many of us have been so distanced from them [due to the not-so-obvious imposition of schooling, that force feeds us certain things (IMPRESSION) while starving us of others (OMISSION) - "out of sight, out of mind"] that their voices have become but faint whispers. What have our ancestors been whispering to us, and where have they been attempting to direct our attention? They've been pointing us to the skull and what's inside. Ok, but why? Might the reason be because this is where the Fountain of Youth is found? The assertion of this book is a resounding and emphatic YES, but let's look at some evidence left by our ancestors that support this (and you decide for yourself).

The beautiful and powerful thing about the clues left to us by our GGs is that the evidence and testimony they provide is not only reliable and trustworthy, but it also allows us to look and see what is right in front of our eyes if we are willing to look and use our noodles to connect the right dots. If we choose to NOT look and see and think, then that is on us (onus), and we will be forced to experience life from a lower perspective and vibration based on incorrect and incomplete perception (continually struggling to "under-stand" while never even inching toward "over-standing").

Let's look and see a few crucial breadcrumbs from ages past left to us by our loving, greatest, and grandest parents.

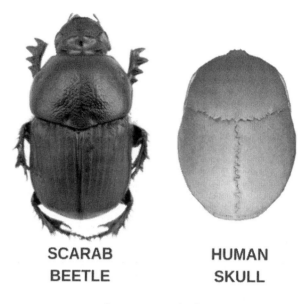

SCARAB BEETLE **HUMAN SKULL**

Image 1.1

THE SCARAB BEETLE WAS SUCH AN IMPORTANT SYMBOL FOR OUR GGs, and it meant/means eternal life, renewal, rebirth, and transformation. Is it any coincidence that the Fountain of Youth happens to carry the exact same meaning? Not only do we receive this clue from our trustworthy GGs who had no incentive to lie to those of us alive today, we can use our own eyes to look and see for ourselves (direct sensory input) that the outer appearance of the scarab beetle is practically identical with that of the human skull when viewed from above (a heavenly perspective). The Bible uses the expressions Golgotha and Calvary to indicate the head region of the human body, which both literally mean "place of the skull." Now that we know where to look (in the skull), let's take a peek at some of the clues our GGs left about what's inside the skull.

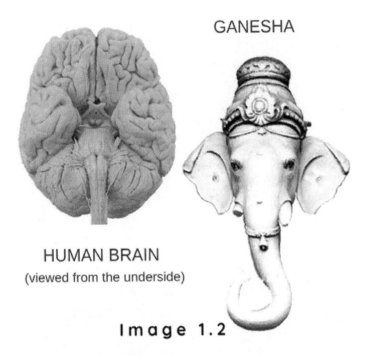

GANESHA

HUMAN BRAIN
(viewed from the underside)

Image 1.2

Our next breadcrumb points directly to the BRAIN. This is an image of Ganesha (or Ganesh), a Hindu deity aptly symbolizing the "remover of obstacles" since it is the brain that, when properly powered, equips us to receive the right ideas and the will to follow those ideas up with corresponding right action (with the strength of an OX). Look closely to find all the features of Ganesha's head and face be revealed in the brain image, especially that of the Cerebellum (which governs voluntary movement), Pons, Midbrain, Medulla Oblongata, and Spinal Cord, although there are many more fine details beyond these parts of the brain that correspond with Ganesh. The important point here is to look and to see what is utterly obvious.

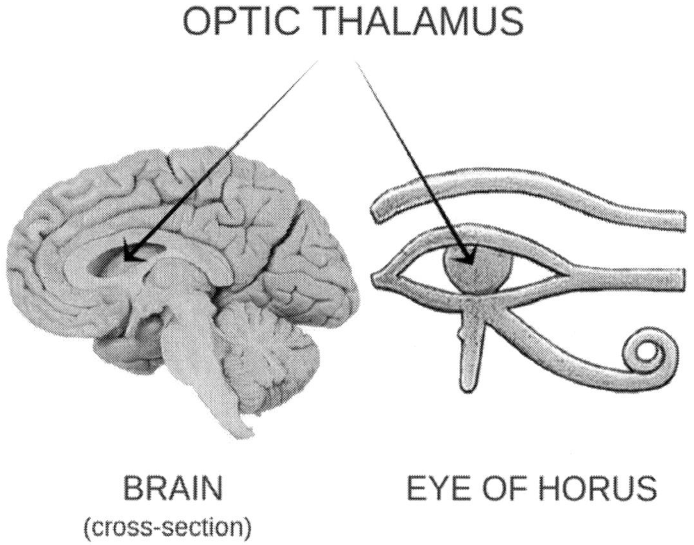

OPTIC THALAMUS

BRAIN
(cross-section)

EYE OF HORUS

Image 1.3

And then there's Horus (in Egyptian cosmology), the son of Isis and Osiris, where the Jesus story of the immaculate conception is said to come from, another breadcrumb. Isis is representative of the Moon energy, Ida (the THA of haTHA yoga), and the pituitary gland. Osiris (notice Os + iris, having to do with the "eye") is representative of the Sun energy, Pingala (the HA of HAtha yoga), and the pineal gland. Horus, aka Heru, is also where the expressions horizon, horoscope, hero, and others come from.

A midsagittal section of the brain shows the symbol represented by the Eye of Horus, and reveals the "optic thalamus," an expression that's modified from the term ophthalmos or ophthalmic. Most today might be familiar with ophthalmology — the branch of modern medicine dealing with the study and treatment of eye diseases (go figure... diseases) — and this reveals the relationship the ophthalmos has with the EYE. The optic thalamus is the ophthalmos, which means "eye" (not eyes). This is "the eye single" the Bible talks about in Matthew 6:22 where it reads "The light of the body is the eye: if therefore thine eye be single, thy whole body shall be full of light."

This is a good time to mention Ptah, which also comes to us from Egyptian cosmology, and literally translates as "opener" or "mouth" or "sculptor." Ptah was worshipped for having profound creative powers (water too is known for its profound creative powers, which is why it's what is sought when trying to determine whether or not life can exist), and sneaks into our conversation here by way of the optic thalamus. When the Greeks took the concept of Ptah as their own, they transliterated it in their alphabet as phi-theta-alpha (which is $\phi\theta\alpha$). Since ϕ (phi) = ph, θ (theta) = th, and α (alpha) = a, this gives PHTHA for Ptah, making it obvious where the spelling for oPHTHAlmos comes from, OR making it obvious that Ptah is directly related to the "eye," take your pick of what's obvious. Perhaps Ptah is also an "eye opener" as well as a "sculptor" (skull + ptah + or, "or/ore" having to do with "gold" which I'll also discuss further in another book).

The ophthalmos or ophthalmic is the optic thalamus, the "eye" or 3rd Eye, the Eye of Horus. It's also important here to note that the word mouth (one of the interpretations of Ptah) was commonly used to refer to the "opening of a river." The Bible speaks of the Jordan River as a metaphor for the spinal cord (the strait, mentioned in KJV Matthew 7:14, through which cerebral spinal fluid or CSF flows). Also, in this metaphor, the brain is the Sea of Galilee and the sacrum is the Dead Sea, where the river empties.

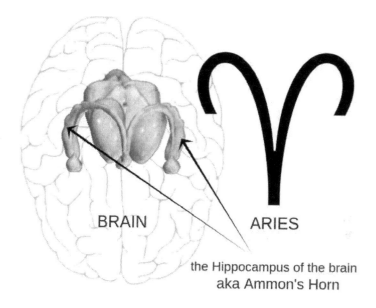

BRAIN   ARIES

the Hippocampus of the brain
aka Ammon's Horn

Image 1.4

The zodiac also reveals itself as a clue left to us by our ancestors, that the brain is of paramount importance. What a lot of people don't know is that the Bible actually encourages its students to know the zodiac, their zodiac, which includes extensive study and knowledge of their natal or birth charts. In Job 38:32 the Bible asks "Canst thou bring forth Mazzaroth in his season? or canst thou guide Arcturus with his sons?" The word mazzaroth, derived from Hebrew, means "zodiac." We must not be fooled just because it isn't written in a language we speak; we must put forth the effort to look into it. And when we say zodiac here, we are NOT talking about silly newspaper horoscopes or any foolishness that has to do with predicting the future, we are talking about the deep science of astrology that developed as man (with and without womb) quested to learn and know Self in order to rise out of her/his animal nature and ascend back to her/his divinity through Self perfection. Astro "light" + logy "the study of" makes astrology literally mean the "study of Light" (Light being literal light, the luminaries in our Sky and Heavens that enable us to see with our two eyes, and the metaphoric light called "knowledge" giving sight to our eye single).

Aries is the first sign of the zodiac represented by the Ram (a male lamb). The arrival of Aries also marks the first season of each year known as Spring, which commences March 21. The hippocampus in the limbic system of brain anatomy is also referred to as Ammon's Horn, and Ammon (also Amon or Amen "the hidden one") is an Egyptian deity represented as a Ram's Head. Even the first three consonants of "limbic" in "limbic system" are LMB (or lamb). The hippocampus is also shaped just like a seahorse. Could the "seahorse" be the ancients' way of whispering to us to SEE HORUS and to know to acknowledge "water" (the fountain of youth, or river) when we say "sea" (sea and see being homonyms)? To add, mare in English means "a female horse," and recall that mare in Latin means "water" (like "sea water"). Hmmm...

In terms of the Fountain of Youth, it should also be noted that... well... if I asked you to fill in the blank — "The Spring begins in _____" — how would you complete that sentence? It's not that you don't already know the Truth about the Fountain of Youth, you just don't remember (re-membering meaning to "put back together" what was dis-membered). Yes, the Spring begins in March (specifically March 21), but another way to respond is the Spring begins in Aries. This statement tells exactly where the Fountain is located, as you will see.

YOGA, Truth, & The Real Fountain of Youth

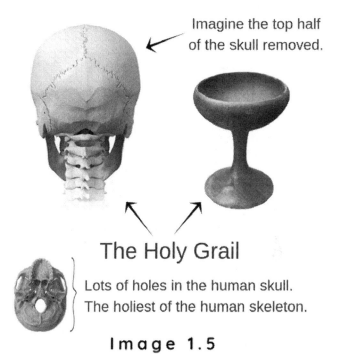

Imagine the top half of the skull removed.

The Holy Grail

Lots of holes in the human skull.
The holiest of the human skeleton.

Image 1.5

Alas, we come to the HOLY GRAIL. The holes of the skull are called foramina (plural) or FORAMEN (singular), which is "for Amen" when you separate out the words in foramen (look and see with your own eyes for direct sensory input and recall what we just mentioned about Amen/Ammon in the previous section). There are many small foramina which allow for tiny nerve canals and blood vessels to pass throughout the skull, and there is one big foramen at the base of the skull called the Foramen Magnum. The skull has many holes in it, making it very HOLY — the HOLIEST of HOLIES.

How do we know the head/skull is the HOLY GRAIL? Well, a first obvious clue is because it is so holy, or filled with holes (again, observe with your own eyes), and that these holes are literally written as "for Amen" (infer and connect the dots). Also, if you remove the Calvarian Cap (as it's known in anatomy, also recalling that Calvary means "place of the skull") from the skull image (in

1.5) on the left, you'll be left with what looks just like the chalice image on the right. Beyond that, the word grail comes from Old French graal which means "cup," and cup comes from Old English cuppe, which comes from PIE keup, whose German cognate kopf now strictly means "head." If we choose, we can also reverse the direction in our etymological search, beginning with head, and get back to grail.

In Old English, skull was heafod-bolla; heafod meaning "head" and bolla meaning "bowl" so literally, the skull was thought of as a "head bowl," and it's the skull that is so holy with all the holes in it. Grail can also be traced to Greek krater which means "bowl," especially that used for mixing wine with WATER — another possible hint toward the Fountain of Youth, as the Bible makes many references to wine and water.

There are many more breadcrumbs out there, but these are some of the most familiar and easily researchable ones that have been dangling in front of us for some time. Remember, it's up to us to look. If we never look, we'll never see. And even if we do look, at first we may not see, if our eyes haven't been properly developed, trained, and prepared to see. But by actively looking ("seeking" — notice SEE+KING) we have initiated/activated a process that will eventually develop our vision to see what we were unable to see before. Just don't let your curiosity be aborted, and keep asking, seeking, and knocking (and soon you will rule over self AS King, when you come to SEE King and KNOW king; "king" being synonymous with kingdom which is king + dome "head" corresponding to the pineal gland).

Part 2

THE FOUNTAIN OF YOUTH & GETTING KNOCKED UP

"This is your last chance. After this, there is no turning back. You take the blue pill - the story ends, you wake up in your bed and believe whatever you want to believe. You take the red pill - you stay in Wonderland and I show you how deep the rabbit hole goes." ~ Morpheus [from the movie The Matrix (1999)]

Damon Givehand

We introduced and investigated some words, ideas, concepts, and artifacts intended to open and prime the mind for our exploration into the Truth about the REAL Fountain of Youth. Now, let's look into and listen to the root meanings of fountain, youth, and yoga, tracing their origins as much as we can, while introducing a few other words and word connections along the way, just like we have been.

♦ THE FOUNTAIN ♦

What does the etymology of the word fountain reveal it means? A fountain, from Old French fontaine, is "a natural SPRING" and regards what "flows" or what "runs." Fountain comes from Latin fons "spring (of water)" plus PIE dhen "to run" or "flow." The vital fluids, vital meaning "of or manifesting life" and fluid meaning "that which flows," of the human body (like: blood, lymph, saliva, cerebrospinal fluid or CSF, etc.) are WATERS that flow throughout the human body. Interestingly, our bodies are almost entirely water, or vital fluid, quite literally making all of us bodies of water. Most of us may have heard that the human body is about 55-75% water give or take (just like our planet Earth), but we may not have been thinking of it like this — that WE are actually "bodies of water." We do, however, think of the Arctic Ocean, Lake Victoria, the Black Sea, the Gulf of Mexico, Salt Lake, and the like as bodies of water.

Also, our blood, at least the liquid portion of it called plasma (about 95% water), is remarkably similar in composition to ocean and sea water. It's as if instead of living in the ocean like whales, dolphins, and walruses, we walk on land and carry our oceans with us and call it blood. When the Bible mentions the Red Sea, it's actually talking about our blood system. The Good Book is all about human physiology, physical regeneration, and becoming WHOLE (thus HOLY Bible, listen to the sound of the words; to walk and exist wholly, whole and intact, is to become holy). And, as mentioned earlier, the Jordan River is a metaphor for the spinal cord, which has CSF circulating through it. Time and time again, water references are being made in the Bible (which is talking about the human body / Earth) — water being the liquid of Life.

Getting back to the fountain, it's the choroid plexuses of the lateral, third, and fourth ventricles of the brain from which the CSF SPRINGs forth, and it's from here that the CSF flows throughout the brain and runs down the spinal cord. Medical terminology lets us know we're talking about water too, by the names it uses for parts of the midbrain, like: cerebral aqueduct, aqueductus mesencephali, sylvian aqueduct, or aqueduct of Sylvius. Notice the word aqueduct. Aqueduct is aqua "water" + duct "course, direction, channel" (from PIE deuk- "to lead" like a duke) meaning the cerebral aqueduct is the channel of our leading, foremost, or chief water, the CSF. To cap it off, CSF is clear (barring no infections of rare conditions) and upwards of 99% water, making it practically nothing but water. The choroid plexuses of the brain's ventricular system are from where the pristine vital waters of CSF spring forth, and from where the waters flow. This spring in the choroid plexus is The Fountain, and since the choroid plexuses are in everyone's brain, the Fountain is in you!

Popular science (the not-so-reliable-or-trustworthy kind of science) teaches that the primary function and purpose of CSF is to provide a cushion protecting the brain from trauma inside the skull's casing. If that was the CSF's "primary" function, that would be inefficient, at best, by whatever we choose to name the grand force of Creation and all its infinite intelligence. While CSF may happen to serve as a buffer for the brain against head trauma, the primary purpose of CSF is undoubtedly way beyond that, being the chief and foremost water of the body, the liquid of Life, as you will see when we get to the brain's uterus.

♦ YOU AND I ♦

The only general, anatomical differences in the human family are with respect to the LOWER reproductive parts of males and females. Beyond that, not only do we all have the same vital fluids coursing through us, which are predominantly water, we also have the same bones and tissues, making you and I physiologically the same in practically every way. The basic physical distinction between us just depends from which perspective we are referring, yours or mine. To me, you are you. But if you were referring to yourself, you'd say I, and if you were referring to me, you'd say you. Make sense? Perspective aside though, you and I are composed of the exact same ingredients, and our bodies undergo and perform the same processes.

We all have blood, spit, urine, aqueous humour, synovial fluid, CSF, plasma, stomach acid, hormonal secretions, tears, etc.; we all have skeletal bones, cartilage, muscle tissue, skin, ligaments, skulls (more bones), and brains, etc.; and we all breathe, poop, pee, digest food, circulate blood, bleed (when cut or scraped), form scabs (when cut or scraped and bleeding), drink, blink, think, dream, sleep, wake up, etc. YOU AND I ARE THE SAME with the same anatomies and "waters" that do the same things. In our brains we see even more of our shared sameness, with the brains of males and females being identical and androgynous (meaning our brains express both "male and female" reproductive organs), varying only in proportionate sizes of different brain parts and amounts of hormonal secretions.

Now that we have that established, that you and I are the same, along with covering the meaning of fountain, let's look into the words youth and yoga.

♦ THE TERMS YOUTH AND YOGA ♦

A peek into the word YOUTH reveals its Old English (OE) roots in geoguð "youth" leading us to the related OE geong "young." In OE the g is said to have had two pronunciations, the soft g as in good and the y as in yes (maybe even pronounced close to "jes"), so we can see the connection shared between youth and geoguð, as well as with young and geong. Geo-, which means earth today (as observed in the terms geography and geometry), would've been pronounced yee-oh very close to our modern jee-oh, where the g would have a slight y sound to it giving us jee+oh+ng for jyung which is "young."

Further, you might already know from any exposure you may have had to foreign languages, that in Spanish the letter y is often pronounced as the j is pronounced in English today (possibly exposing the bridged, often blended, sound of j and y in OE, like the Spanish double LLs giving the jy sound as we wrote for jyung before). Therefore, the Spanish word yo, which means "I," is often pronounced like the English joe. In the previous paragraph, we saw geo- pronounced yee-oh close to jee-oh, which said rapidly becomes joe, just like the Spanish word yo for I. This is a key connection to why when reading the Bible, when the word Earth is encountered, it's often referring to the human body — your body. As the reader of the Bible, you are the me or the I doing the reading in "first person" (even the letter I looks like the number 1 for "first" person, and is homonyms with eye meaning "that which sees"). As the I doing the reading, you are the yo (Spanish), the geo or Earth, a body of water, your body. This is one way the Bible refers to the human body - your human body (and mine) - as Earth, by way of parable and equivocation, and as evidenced by geo- or yo ("joe") for I.

Going even further, now that we've linked yo with OE geo, yoga can be re-written as geo-ghah for closer analysis. Ghah is the 16th letter of the Ancient Hebrew alphabet (the Modern Hebrew Ayin) whose early symbol was an eye meaning "to watch, know." Today, ghah often shows up as separate from ayin (which now holds the 16th letter position by itself) and appears like an add-on to the modern Hebrew alphabet. Interestingly, the nineteenth letter of the Arabic alphabet is ghayn, as if a blend between ghah and ayin. In any event, the modern Hebrew ghah is represented by a symbol that looks like two strands of rope twisted around each other (like DNA), and means "dark, wicked." If geo-ghah (yoga) is geo/yo "I/earth" + ghah "eye" (as in the Heavenly ophthalmos "eye") — perhaps this is what our Rastafarian brothers mean when we hear them say "I and I" (that it's actually "I and Eye") — then these are what we must learn to yoke or join together into one whole, in order that "thine eye be single" (from Matthew 6:22) so that the whole body will be full of light, rather than the darkness/wickedness that's said to be symbolized by modern Hebrew's ghah.

Another peculiar and observable fact (for anyone to see whose eyes are open and ready) is that the first two letters of the word you are y and o, or yo which means "I." Here we can see through the spelling that I am in YOU since I and YO are interchangeable. U (meaning "you" as we typically understand that term to mean today) and I are wrapped up in one with the expression YOU. You and I are one and the same.

And yet another interesting fact revealed when researching the etymology of youth, is that the medial g in the OE geoguð became the letter yogh, probably pronounced very close to "yoke" with the gh (in yogh) sounding like a throat-clearing "k" or "h" going to the root meaning of yoga (although many linguists, while they admit they don't know and are only giving their best guesses, like to believe yogh was pronounced like "yock" rhyming with our modern English lock with a throat-clearing kh sound like the German ch sound after a, o, u, or au, sounding like lach in Loch Ness monster, while pronouncing the o with perhaps more of an Irish or Scottish accent). The argument could even be made for yogh becoming yoke+ha then yog+ha then yoga based on the same matter discussed earlier with the g and k in terms of prek — for prek-nant and prek-unta.

In short, there are some striking and intriguing connections between and within the terms you, youth, and yoga that are more than worth noting, and the connections do not end there. As we saw already in the section titled THE BIBLE AND YOGA FIT LIKE HAND-IN-GLOVE, PIE gives yeug- as meaning "to join, to yoke," which is the same as the Sanskrit root for yoga, yuj "to yoke, to join, to unite." Interestingly, PIE yeu- without the ending g in yeug-, is pronounced like modern English you, and means "vital force." Being alive, YOU are loaded with vital force, you must be, otherwise you'd be dead. In fact, you are the epitome of vital force. Since you and I are the same, I too am packed with vital force, and epitomize it — I am yeu- (do you hear it? "I am you"). We are all brimming with yeu. And wouldn't you know, it happens that the practice of yoga (like Qigong / Tai Chi) functions to optimize the flow of yeu (in you and I), although referred to as prana (or chi). Remember that yeu- is the root of yeug, revealing that "vital force" is integral in yoga (the process of yoking).

♦ THE TH SUFFIX OF YOU ♦

Consider the terms truth, growth, warmth, and health. According to etymonline.com, the suffix -th "marks the accomplishment of the notion of the base." The bases of truth, growth, warmth, and health, are true, grow, warm, and heal, respectively. So, the -th suffix means the notions underlying being true, growing, being warm, and healing have been accomplished. With this thinking in mind, the word YOUTH suggests that the notion of YOU (being a body of water or vital fluid, and you being yeu "vital force") has been accomplished. You are the human embodiment and manifestation of vital force, and word deconstruction shows that YOUTH is yeu "vital force" + th "marking the accomplishment of the notion of the base" which in this case is yeu. So, we are talking about the accomplishment of the notion of "vital force" (yeu/you). [SIDE NOTE: Consider that EARTH = EAR + TH, marking the accomplishment of the notion of EAR (the base), the notion having to do with what is heard, which is SOUND, as symbolized with Aum/Om. Even KJV John 1:1 reads "In the beginning was the Word, and the Word was with God, and the Word was God" (although this verse goes deeper than sound as it's commonly understood, even in esoteric circles, taking us to the "seed" of Creation)].

Recall that etymology shows the connection between youth and young, both having the root you/yeu ("vital force"). Remember also that you and I are mostly water, making the link between water and staying young ("sustained with vital force") evident. Hopefully, this connection alone will, at the very least, be enough to get people to drink more water — clean, living water, herbal teas, and fresh juice from truly organic fruits, greens, and vegetables (which is nothing but water that has been filtered through those plants); NOT tap water, which is more often than not fluoridated, or commercial water with additives and "enhancers." BEWARE of believing the hype about fluoride, which, the way it's administered to people through tap water, has a calcifying effect on the pineal gland, an integral and significant part of your third eye anatomy (which this book doesn't go deep into directly, but you are encouraged to research further and syncretize it with what you learn here).

♦ IT'S IN EWE ♦

(KJV) ST. JOHN 4:14
But whosoever drinketh of the water that I shall give him shall never thirst; but the water that I shall give him shall be IN HIM a well of water springing up into everlasting life.

OK, now it's time to LISTEN to the word pronounced like the English "you" to be prepared to grasp the meaning of the statement ...the fountain of youth is IN you. Say the word you out loud to yourself, and just listen. Next, read and say the English word ewe out loud. What did you notice? What was the difference in the pronunciations of these words? If you pronounced these two words (you and ewe) correctly, then you should have found no difference at all in their pronunciations. These two words are phonetically identical, meaning they are homonyms, they sound alike. Homonym = homo "same" + nym "name," and names are what we "call" things, what we speak or say. In the beginning was the word/sound. Also, NAME is an anagram for AMEN "the hidden one" which is "IN you" as well. The words you and ewe are the exact same word, aka sound, or name as we've just learned. This will make more sense by the end, just keep in mind that the word you can be replaced with the word ewe.

At this time, observe the first three consonants of the word limbic, as in the limbic system of the brain, and see LMB, standing for lamb. [SIDE NOTE: Hebrew, like many other ancient languages, understood vowels, but did not write them, as they were considered to be "vows to EL" (EL being the Hebrew word for God).] Now, revisit the statement "...the fountain of youth is in you" and look at it again as "...the fountain of youth is IN EWE." This is the parable, as the female lamb is called a ewe, yet the brain "above" is androgynous (expressing both male and female parts, i.e. the ram and the ewe). In other words the fountain of youth is IN THE LAMB (the Ram — remember the hippocampus, Ammon's Horn?). [SIDE NOTE: Funny how the part of the human brain known for memory is the limbic system (LMB), and in the computer world, computer memory is called RAM or Random Access Memory. Coincidence? You decide.] What the Bible calls the Lamb of God, this is in you/ewe, the choroid plexus of your androgynous brain. It's in all of us, every single human being alive. [SIDE NOTE: Brings a new perspective to the 1991 film The Silence of The Lambs, with the serial killer Hannibal Lecter eating the brains of his victims, now doesn't it? What is the hidden message and deeper meaning of that movie and WHY that title? …doubtful that it has anything to do with Clarice as a youngster hearing the screaming of lambs about to be slaughtered.]

Even the verse at the start of this section, (KJV) St. John 4:14, is letting us know that the fountain that bestows everlasting life is IN US by saying "… IN HIM…" when referring to "…whosoever drinketh of the water…" (don't forget that Bible means "to absorb, soak in, to drink in, inhale," from Latin bibō "drink"). While the Bible speaks in parables, it speaks plainly, as we've been witnessing, so that we may sip from its wisdom and fill our cups (heads, Holy Grails) once we are ready, having spiritually ripened enough. Now, let's revisit "you and I" being the same, but this time it's "ewe and eye" that are the same.

♦ EWE AND EYE ♦

(KJV) MATTHEW 6:22
The light of the body is the eye: if therefore thine eye be single, thy whole body shall be full of light.

And...

(KJV) REVELATION 21:23
And the city had no need of the sun, neither of the moon, to shine in it: for the glory of God did lighten it, and the Lamb is the light thereof.

We've already established that you and I are the same. Now let's show that EWE and EYE are likewise the same. In (KJV) Matthew 6:22, it's stated in straight forward fashion that "...the light of the body is the eye." Then just as plainly in (KJV) Revelation 21:23 it says "...the Lamb is the light thereof" ("the light thereof" being the Lamp of the body — note how close the pronunciations of lamb and lamp are, and how close in shape the symbols b and p are; not even to mention that in Middle High German lamb actually means "lamp," straight up). If the light of the body is the eye, and the Lamb is the light, then the eye is the Lamb (ram or ewe) according to the basic mathematical axiom (generally credited to Euclid), which states that "things which are equal to the same thing are equal to each other." Keep in mind that "is" means "equals," and equals means "exactly the same as," NOT mostly alike or similar. So, in others terms, if A=B and C=A, then B=C; meaning B and C are the exact same. Therefore, if THE LIGHT is THE EYE and THE LAMB is THE LIGHT, then THE EYE and THE LAMB (a ewe being a lamb) are equal to each other since they both equal the light. So EWE = EYE, meaning EWE and EYE are the exact same!

Further, the Eye of Horus symbol can be seen in the midsagittal section of the brain (as shown earlier in Image 1.3), and when the image of that same area of the brain is viewed from the front we can see the Lamb (or Ram) of the limbic (LMB) system. The EYE (of Horus) and the Lamb (of God), or EWE, are the same. EWE and EYE are the same. The Fountain of Youth is in EWE can now be thought of as "The Fountain of Youth is in EWE and EYE." Now it should be evident why at the beginning of this book, when it read "If I was to tell you in your ear where the fountain of youth is, you'd hear '...the fountain of youth is in you and I,' I'd be sharing a profound truth with you in the most direct and explicit way, yet the words uttered would not convey what you are about to read, in even the minutest way; not because the spoken words '...the fountain of youth is in you and I' aren't clear, but because you, the hearer, have been trained to hear in one predominant and predictable way." At this point, it is hoped that you appreciate what was said in the beginning and you now hear that statement in an entirely new way, that the fountain of youth is in ewe and eye, and understand fully what this means unconfounded by equivocation. By now you should also see why others won't be able to grasp the depth of what you mean if you were to whisper this same Truth in their ears.

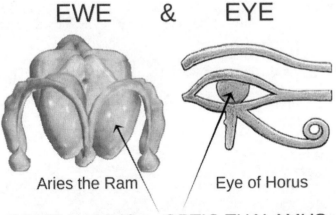

EWE & EYE

Aries the Ram — Eye of Horus

OPHTHALMUS or OPTIC THALAMUS

Both the EWE (or Lamb of God) and the EYE refer to the same region of the brain, the DIENCEPHALON ("God Head"), which is revealed by the oPHTHAlmus.

Image 2.1

As if what we've already been covering hasn't been interesting enough, HERE'S WHERE IT BEGINS TO GET REALLY FRICKIN' INTERESTING if we are willing to THINK and connect the right dots right before our eyes, considering everything we now know up to this point based on what we've covered.

What is the meaning of the word ewe? A ewe is a lamb, specifically a female lamb, which may become pregnant unlike the ram that's male. In the center of the brain, the same area as the lateral, third, and fourth ventricles, AND the cerebral aqueduct, is the limbic system. When isolated and viewed from certain aspects, the limbic system looks just like a ram (a male lamb, but always remember that the brain is androgynous, meaning it expresses both male and female reproductive parts). When viewing the limbic system straight on, especially and primarily the ventricles (which is where the choroid plexuses are), it's also part of what looks just like a UTERUS (a uterus being where pregnancy takes place) — see Image 2.2.

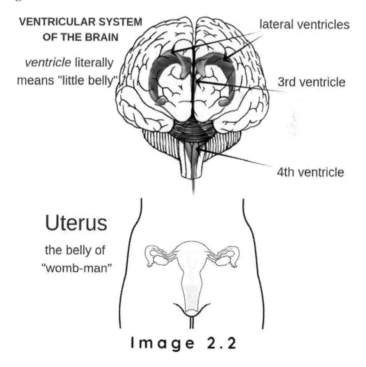

Image 2.2

♦ THE BRAIN'S UTERUS: AS ABOVE ♦

What most people today aren't aware of is that we humans are all men. Man with womb is called "womb-man" while man without womb is just called "man." Instead of recognizing this fact, most of us unwittingly get ensnared in divisive, sexist, gender thinking. That said, in the typical pregnancy with which most of us are probably familiar, the fetus develops in the womb, also known as the uterus. Within the womb, the fetus is enclosed by an outer membrane called the chorion combined with an inner membrane called the amnion, together forming the amniotic sac which holds the nourishing and growth-promoting amniotic fluid. As the fetus grows and as the amniotic fluid continues to accumulate, the sac expands while the belly of the womb-man swells until the sac eventually ruptures — or "water breaks" — labor is undergone, and birth is given.

Our ancient GG's told us "as above so below" NOT "as below so above." What happens below is a reflection of what happens above not vice versa. So, this pregnancy (remember pregunta and preknant from Part 1, AND ask, seek, knock) that happens in the brain, shows up in the lower reproductive parts of man. The names of parts and processes most of us might be familiar with in the lower regions, are actually named after the parts and processes that come from the higher region above, in the brain (but school completely omits this from the education it force spoon feeds, which is a form of blatant censorship, and this Truth never dawns on people, preventing people from learning about and knowing their own true power which is literally a "higher" power). The lower is named after the higher, although it might seem the other way around since schools don't teach about ABOVE. Yet, most of us are somewhat, if not thoroughly, aware of the BELOW parts and processes!

The first paragraph of this section describes what happens

BELOW in the lower generative regions of man when bringing forth life. Now, let's correlate that with ABOVE and what's in the beautiful androgynous brain. Remember, the CSF springs forth and flows from the lateral, third, and fourth ventricles of the choroid plexus, although predominantly from the 3rd ventricle (which, you guessed it, is part of the 3rd Eye). The etymology of choroid reveals it means "like a chorion," so choroid likewise means "outer membrane of the embryo or fetus sac" or "membrane enclosing the embryo or fetus" which together with an amnion contains amniotic fluid, but this time it's in the brain. Being that choroid indicates an amniotic sac, it implies the potential conception, development, and birth of a fetus that happens as a result of pregnancy, also in the brain. If you look, you will also find in this same part of the brain, something referred to as the embryonic neural cavity, which develops into the ventricular system (just more word evidence, supporting the existence of a uterus in the brain because it's referring to an "embryo," although some may try to mistakenly argue that embryonic in this case indicates it's a cavity that develops in us when we are embryos).

Additionally, the word amnós, from which the terms amnion and amniotic (fluid) are derived, means "lamb," lending further support to the notion of The Lamb of God in the brain center. The limbic system (LMB) is also in the brain center and includes the diencephalon (where diencephalon literally means "God head" as Old French dieu means "God" and cephalon means "head"). Notice too, that the first three letters of amnós (amnion and amniotic) are AMN or Amen "the hidden one" casting another angle of light on the hidden meaning and purpose of the Foramen Magnum at the base of the skull through which the medulla oblongata becomes the spinal cord (recall that Foramen = "For Amen").

Could the CSF of the choroid plexus be the constructive and rejuvenating amniotic water of the Fountain of Youth restoring everlasting life? BUT OF COURSE! The "Lamb of God" is literally the "Amnion of the Diencephalon." Even the word fetus, which by definition is what is held and developed in a choroid/chorion (whose inner lining is amnion), alludes to YES. Fetus literally means "offspring" and offspring literally means "of or from SPRING." And, as we already covered, spring means "source of a stream, river, or flow of water rising and bursting forth" while fountain means "a natural spring." This natural spring of water is the amniotic fluid of the brain, and amniotic fluid develops in uteruses.

♦ THE EWE-TAURUS ♦

The cerebellum governs motor control and the coordination of voluntary movements (like balance, speech, posture, etc.). The cerebellum also corresponds with TAURUS (the Bull) the second sign of the zodiac right after Aries (the Ram/Lamb/Ewe, the first zodiac sign). The Bull has to do with tremendous strength in action and muscular activity, like the kind of strength it takes for yoked oxen to plow the field so the seed can be sown. Once you know how to look and listen (pratyaksha "direct sensory input"), just as you can see and hear the RAM in cerebrum, given that cerebrum = Sara + AbRAM (from Genesis in the Bible — GENEsis meaning "generation, origin, nativity, creation" coming from gignesthai "to be born" and PIE gen- / gene "give birth"; gene also having to do with DNA), you can also see and hear the BULL in cereBELLum with cereBULLum. Both bell and bull (and even bowl, going back to the skull as the chalice or Holy Grail) are etymologically traced back to PIE bhel- "to sound, roar, blow, SWELL." Then, when you look up the etymology of TORUS (homonyms with TAURUS), you find it means "SWELLing" or "bulge" (BULLge) just like you find in pregnant BELLies.

When looking below at the UTERUS (in the lower reproductive organ of the womb-man), you will observe what strongly resembles a ram's head, with the horns being the fallopian tubes, and the uterine tube being the length of the ram's face. In the brain you see the same shape with the fornix and hippocampus on each side, essentially encapsulated by the lateral ventricles, forming the horns of the ram. In brain anatomy the Hippocampus is also referred to as Ammon's Horn(s), and in Egyptian cosmology Ammon (Amon or Amen) is depicted with a Ram's head.

In the brain's uterus, the fourth ventricle is located in the place often thought of as the womb in the lower reproductive parts (although womb and uterus are often considered essentially synonymous), and the cereBULLum is the roof of the fourth ventricle of the brain. Ventricle means "little belly," coming from Latin ventris "belly." Belly, like bell, bull, and bowl, can also be traced back to bhel- "to SWELL" as well as PIE bhelgh- "to SWELL" and bholgh- "bulge" (BULLge). Not only is the bull traditionally recognized as a symbol of virility, strength, transformation, and fulfillment by many elder cultures, it also symbolizes fertility, making it an easy connection with "SWELLing" or "bulging" (BULLging) like a pregnant BELLy.

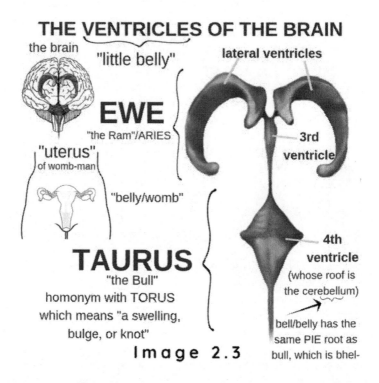

Image 2.3

The lateral, third, and fourth ventricles, and the surfaces of surrounding parts of the brain that make up the ventricular walls, together form the EWE-TAURUS (uterus) of the brain. This is where the pregnancy in the brain takes place whereby we may be born again into everlasting life. So, have church and ask (preguntas), seek, and knock, or get pregnant (which is KNOcked up or KNOwing)!

♦ THE LIVING FOUNTAIN REVEALED ♦

(KJV) REVELATIONS 7:17
For the Lamb which is in the midst of the throne shall feed them, and shall lead them unto living fountains of waters: and God shall wipe away all tears from their eyes.

Interesting that this verse has "...living fountains of waters..." in it. Well, it's the living fountain of water in each of us to which this book is dedicated. And we are informed by this verse, or it is "revealed" to us (thus it's in the chapter called REVELATIONS), that when fed by the Lamb (the purified amniotic CSF or Virgin Mary) we will be led to living fountains of waters whereby our suffering shall cease. As if we are asking that the Lamb "feed us" (which sounded out is "fetus").

Aside from grasping the parables and recognizing the personified and storified physiological processes of the human body/temple, a huge challenge many face when it comes to comprehending the Bible, is they read words that appear familiar and mistakenly believe those words to mean what they've always unconsciously assumed them to mean without investigation or examination. People are wise to remember that the KJV Bible was translated from its original Hebrew (Old Testament) and Greek (New Testament) into an English that straddles a time of transition from Middle English to Early Modern English, and what we understand English words to mean today may not be exactly the same as 400 or 500 years ago. The outer shell of word spellings may look the same while the words' meanings may have changed (or at least be significantly different than we unconsciously assume).

Let's look into some key words from this verse with the intent of decoding it...

LAMB = amnós (literally meaning "lamb") relating to the

amnion, the "lining of the amniotic sac" which carries the fetus "offspring" in the lateral, third, and fourth ventricles "little bellies" of the brain, and is where CSF (cerebrospinal fluid) is produced — in the choroid plexus

MIDST = "middle"

THRONE = "elevated seat," seat is a "place, occupied by a sovereign" (sover "super/over" + reign "to rule as a king with royal authority" or like a "lord, master" as in kyrios, taking us back to church; as the sovereign part of ourselves), this is the part of us that "rules over our actions" (OVER the cerebellum), it "rules over our choices and decisions," this part of us is located in the head/brain region inside the skull (without getting into the pineal body being representative of the king, and the pituitary gland that of the queen, which corresponds to the locations of the king's and queen's chambers of the Great Pyramid; to witness how the pineal gland shows up in the Bible, see KJV Genesis 32:30 where it's spelled Peniel)

MIDST OF THE THRONE = "middle of the head"

SHALL = "will have to, must (because under obligation), obligated, obliged"

FEED = "nourish, sustain"

LEAD = "march at the head of as a guide" (notice the word "march" and keep in mind that March 21st is when the Spring commences and the first Zodiac sign, Aries — the Ram — is ushered in)

UNTO = "until, up to, as far as"

LIVING = "having life" where life means "vitality," which is "vital force" i.e. yeu; living indicates a condition where the notion of yeu "vital force" has been accomplished and is continually being carried out, therefore the suffix -th may be applied giving yeu + th, which is youth (or ewe + th)

LIVING FOUNTAINS OF WATERS = Fountains of Youth

GOD = Dieu (Old French); in the brain center is the diencephalon, which is dieu "God" + cephalon " head"

WIPE = "cleanse, purify" or "to make virgin" where the word virgin means "pure"

AWAY = "without delay" as in "right away" or "immediately"

WIPE AWAY = "cleanse, purify, make virgin immediately, without delay"

TEAR = "nectar, fluid from the eye" (amrita, ambrosia, etc...); and nectar comes from nek "death" + tere "crossover, overcome," making tears "fluid from the Eye that bestows everlasting Life."

EYE = ophthalmos (optic thalamus, from which the tears drop or the nectar drops)

TRANSLATION: The choroid plexus, which is in the middle of the head, will nourish and sustain them, and march them up to the FOUNTAIN OF YOUTH: and the Nectar Of Everlasting Life produced in the optic thalami shall be purified immediately in/by the diencephalon.

After decoding this verse alone, we can see it's all about the brain center, with the choroid plexus, diencephalon, optic thalamus (or ophthalmos), and its reference to the "midst of the throne" meaning "middle of the head."

Damon Givehand

Part 3

INTRACOURSE: LOOKING BACKWARD & FORWARD

Damon Givehand

♦ELABORATING YOGA, YOUTH, & TRUTH IN REVIEW♦

Yoga means "to yoke, join, bring together" or "union" OR "TO MAKE WHOLE." The root of yoga is the Sanskrit yuj or PIE yeug. The Sanskrit root of yuj is yu and means "joining, binding, mixing, fastening." The PIE root of yeug is yeu and means "vital force." These meanings of yu and yeu, although to some may seem different, are not different since the essence of what you (and I) are is joined and inextricably mixed with vital force and fluid. It is vital force that mixes throughout us, joining, binding, and fastening us together (the parts of us that are seen, the parts of us that are unseen, that in us which sees, and the seeing process itself) so tightly that we cannot distinguish the seen (and unseen), the seer, and seeing apart from one another (without the application of prolonged special effort — this is a dilemma yoga aims to address and resolve, preparing us to be fit enough to see ALL just as it is).

As can be witnessed with a little investigation of the words YOUTH and YOGA, the essential meanings of the two are inseparably related. Remember that youth is you + th, where the suffix -th means "the notion of the base has been accomplished;" and since you can be substituted with yu ("joining, binding, mixing, fastening") and yeu ("vital force"), youth indicates that the notion of a "fastening vital force" has been accomplished (for which the same can be said of ewe + th). Further, yu/yeu, whose Sanskrit equivalent is prana ("life force"), is also the root of yuj/yeug, which is the root of yoga. So yu/yeu, going to the core of the meaning of "youth," is actually "the root of the root" of yoga.

The yu/yeu in you (and I) springs forth from and in ewe. Yu, yeu, you, and ewe are all homonyms, meaning they all share the "same name" — they represent the same spoken word (sound). Being of the same name, the ideas contained in these words are linked, and linked for a reason by our GGs. When searching for the possible existence of life, popular scientists today use water as the essential ingredient sought. If there is no water, there can be no life. This is because water is the universal vital fluid necessary for the birth of life and the sustenance of life, which is yeu.

CSF is essentially all water, and is recognized as the foremost, chief water of the human being. This watery vital force (yeu) springs forth in the choroid plexuses of the brain and is designated to "feed us" (aka fetus). There are choroid plexuses in each of the four ventricles ("little bellies") of the brain, and bellies are what swell with amniotic fluid as fetuses are developed during pregnancy (this is what the Bible is talking about when it refers to children). When certain conditions are met in the CSF and brain, as a result of "having church" — asking (preguntas), seeking, and knocking — we get "knocked up" with KNOwing, the great quest(ion) of Life. This pregnancy in the brain "may" occur in the EWE-TAURUS (the lateral, third, and fourth ventricles of the brain forming the ventricular system), it just depends on whether we are living Right.

Truth is syncretic, and syncretism is the reconciliation of different views and perspectives, where to reconcile means "to bring into harmony or friendliness again." Note the word again in the previous sentence, as if there was a time when all was already conciliated, harmonious, friendly, and extant in a state of thriving, symbiotic compatibility. Yoga means "to yoke" or "join together." So, Truth being syncretic, is yogic, since syncretism involves bringing or joining together into harmony just as yoga does. Therefore, it also follows (flows) that TRUTH IS WHOLE, since, like yoga, it joins together to form ONE (which is WHOLE, not a fraction or a part).

Truth, then, which fits the apparently separate pieces of Life's puzzle into a whole, UNIversal picture, relies on seeing (or perceiving) correctly which relies on a corrected mind (that without all the pieces cannot be whole or "piece + full" aka peaceful "full of peace"). Since mind is the lens, and the lens becomes covered with the film of deep, pervading, general confusion, due to the mind's nature and having been born into the world, it's in need of being corrected. This confusion is known in the realm of yoga as avidya — a state of deep and pervading confusion whereby we don't know, and we don't know we don't know, and even when we think we know, we still don't know and don't know it. Marinate on that.

Anyone who does not deliberately set out on a quest to correct her or his own mind is under the delusion and influence of avidya, whether they acknowledge it or not, no matter how much they appear to have it all together. A corrected mind does not come about by chance or accident. So we must correct the mind to see Right, which is required to see Truth. Correcting the mind involves the removal of lies, moving us from OBLIVIOUS to seeing the OBVIOUS which this book has attempted to facilitate at least to the minutest degree. The study and application of Patañjali's Yoga Sūtras is how to expedite the correction of the mind so we may reverse engineer and undo the effects of avidya in our lives.

From Patañjali's Yoga Sūtras we get the three criteria for seeing or perceiving correctly (pramāna) which are: 1) direct sensory input (pratyaksha), 2) competent inference (anumāna), and 3) reliable and trustworthy reference(s) (āgamāha). Throughout this book, a primary objective has been to adhere to these three criteria, so as to present irrefutable evidence of the Fountain of Youth without jumping to wild, baseless, and detached conclusions.

For instance, by the first criterion of correct perception, direct sensory input, we were able to use our eyes to look and see that the superior view of the scarab beetle is practically identical with the human skull when viewed from above. We were also able to identify and listen to the sounds of words, like Bible and parables, and hear "bi bull" and "pair of bulls;" then by application of the second criterion, competent inference, we were able to directly connect the Bible with the notion of "yoking" or yoga. Continuing this approach in our investigation, we likewise observed more obvious homonyms like you, yeu, and ewe, as well as I and eye, and by anumāna, connected these words with each other, yoga, the Bible, and the Fountain of Youth. The connections made in this book, like exposing the mirroring realities of ABOVE and BELOW with the ewe-taurus and uterus, while sticking to the first two principles of correct perception, go on and on. And it is by applying pratyaksha and anumāna, that we are able to confidently establish the reliability and trustworthiness of the Bible and other artifacts left to us from the past, which are represented by the third criterion, āgamāha.

♦ THE FOUNTAIN OF YOUTH ♦

The Fountain of Youth is in ewe and eye. The Fountain of Youth is a spring of water, of which anyone who drinks or bathes will become young again, renewed, and even be granted Everlasting Life. Where does this SPRING begin? The SPRING begins in Aries, or the Lamb of God, which is (or is in) the limbic system of the brain center — recall that the first three consonants of limbic are LMB for "lamb." The water is CSF and must be purified, or made VIRGIN. The word for "water" or "sea water" in Latin is mare (pronounced mä'-rā, close to Mary, more or less, depending on where you're from). In English a mare (pronounced mār) is a "female horse" pointing us back to the hippocampus in the androgynous brain (hippo- means "horse"), which appears almost identical to a "sea horse" of the actual sea, living in "sea water." PIE mari also means "sea" or "of the sea." Mare and mari are referred to as MARY in the Bible and can be observed in words like marine and maritime.

When this cerebrospinal water has been purified it's called Virgin Mary (virgin "pure or purified" and mari "water"). As the leading, foremost, and chief water of our bodies, if we are able to live consistent with ways that purify our CSF and keep it pure, then we will be led to living fountains of waters (as revealed in KJV Revelations 7:17), and "may" be granted access to all the benefits of the Fountain of Youth (may means "am able" but doesn't necessarily mean that the ability is put to use — this is not a passive venture, and therefore not a guarantee). Even the word immaculate, from the Immaculate Conception of the Virgin Mary, means "not spotted or defiled" in any way whatsoever, so we have our work cut out if we wish to be led to the living waters of the Fountain of Youth.

We must learn how to cleanse and remain clean; learn what to eat and drink and what to never eat and drink; identify all unhealthy habits and undo them, while replacing them with right, wholesome habits; learn to always exercise total sovereignty over our minds (thoughts and emotions); always do right; learn to love ALL; learn to not worry; and learn to be patient. See, as KJV Matthew 7:14 informs us when it says "Because strait is the gate, and narrow is the way, which leadeth unto life, and few there be that find it," we really do have our work cut out for us!

♦ NOW WHAT? WHAT'S NEXT? ♦

The next reasonable and all-important question to ask is: How can we be granted the powers of this fountain and experience its benefits? If we're not asking this question, then what's the point of the light this book sheds? For some of us, the idea that the Fountain of Youth is real is just too far out there to wrap our heads around and accept, which is fine because we are not all ready at the same time. We each become ready in our own time, like the ripening of fruit. Yet, for others of us, the proof our GGs left for our observance makes it pretty clear that the Fountain of Youth is absolutely real. And even better than that, we can enjoy what our fountains have in store for us, just as our GGs did, all we must do is remember how to live accordingly.

And while I may not be able to irrefutably say for certain exactly what it looks like when we access the powers of our fountains of youth OR what happens when we do, something in me seems to know it has to do with more than just looking young and prolonging life — it involves unlocking our fullest human potentialities (something the current world construct seems hellbent on suppressing). The hope of this book is and has been to pique your curiosity (inspire church in you) so intensely that you'll let nothing stand in your way and stop you from asking, seeking, knocking, and finding out for yourself. If this book has not accomplished that goal, at the very minimum, the hope is that a seed has been firmly planted so that one day you will be ready.

In the event that you are ready (or ready-ish) and you are wondering what you can do to bathe in, bask, or drink from the fountain and be blessed by its gifts and everlasting life, keep in mind there is no doubt that PERFECT HEALTH is where to begin. True health takes SELF-CONTROL, which the world has conditioned us into not exercising. We cannot expect the road ahead to be without great challenge, internal and external, especially since we are breaking new ground with no known modern predecessors to lean on for specific advice and guidance (other than decoding what our GGs left us and re-membering). As already mentioned earlier, we are put on notice of the great challenge ahead by KJV Matthew 7:14. And even though we may not know exactly everything to do at the moment, by this time, based on the presentation of this book, we should know that it CAN be done, because our ancestor GGs obviously knew from experience how to do it. If they were doing it, we can once again figure it out (like our GGs did) if we learn to work together in harmony (like our GGs did). WE CAN REMEMBER.

While everything there is to know on how to activate our fountains of youth may not be known at this moment, due to all the corruption for over at least the past 1500-2000 years (especially the last 500), the following section shares some ideas on where to begin that are obvious starting points for eyes that are prepared to see, based on the context of this book. More will be shared in the edited, revised version of this book and other forthcoming books (based on continued research, continued personal exploration, continued reader feedback and insights, and any collaborations with other researchers in this or related areas, etc.), so stay tuned. For updates in this area, visit damongivehand.com and join my Inner Circle.

(KJV) JOHN 3:12
If I have told you earthly things, and ye believe not, how shall ye believe, if I tell you of heavenly things?

♦THE PRACTICAL EARTHLY THINGS WE CAN ALL DO♦

The Fountain of Youth is what we call a heavenly thing, whereas health of the physical body is an earthly thing. We must take great care of our earth (our physical body, our geo, yo, I) over which we've been given responsibility before we can even hope to ascend to anything heavenly, which calls for us to be significantly MORE responsible. Far too many of us suffer from lack of health, or compromised health, which is a blatant display of being irresponsible with something so precious. Even those of us who are presumably healthy (exhibiting the appearance of health) fall way short of health excellence that approaches purity, a sign that, while somewhat responsible, we are yet not responsible enough (ignorance is no excuse). For instance, it makes no sense to exercise all week to be physically fit with a "good looking body" and then go party and drink alcohol on the weekends. Alcohol inTOXICates the body and destroys health but doesn't prevent someone from "appearing healthy" because of their physically fit "appearance." Health and fitness are not exactly the same thing. Ideally, we want both, but most today opt for fitness over True Health, which reflects the irresponsible, lower, materialistic nature of people, and spiritual immaturity.

We all know that health is important, yet the awareness of its importance too often doesn't translate into health becoming an absolute priority in people's lives. When health becomes an absolute priority, it becomes simple and uncomplicated, and we can no longer be confused by dis- and misinformation. This level of knowing requires us to RETHINK EVERYTHING, even the stuff we thought we figured out already. Remember that the meaning of health has to do with "being whole." When health becomes an absolute priority, we will do whatever we must do to deprogram, reboot, and reprogram ourselves to be oriented toward health in ALL things so we may heal and be whole.

I've been coaching people on how to reclaim, maintain, and optimize their health since about 2006, by sharing with them what I first had to learn, figure out, and do for myself once I made my health an absolute priority. Because I have lived on both sides of health, and now consciously choose to give my all to live continuously on the right side of it (in body, mind, soul, and spirit), I fervently support all others who may be at an earlier stage along the same journey (because I know how challenging it is), and offer some suggestions on where to begin to move in the right direction toward purifying the waters sooner and more rapidly, thereby priming our fountains. If you happen to be at an earlier stage of your health journey, along with the tips offered in the next section (the 9 Divine Suggestions), you are encouraged to read My Fat Story (at damongivehand.com) and another one of my books that goes into a little greater depth and detail regarding health, it's called — OPTIMUM HEALTH MINDSET (OHM): How to Think to Undo Fat, Maximize Your Vitality, and Never Get Sick Again.

Before we can hope to bask in the waters of the Fountain of Youth, we must first make health an absolute priority, by cleansing and purifying our Temples (bodies/earth), thus proving our worthiness. If we are not willing to clean and purify our bodies, then the Fountain of Youth will remain a fairy tale. The hope is that by learning about the True existence of the Fountain of Youth, there will be strong incentive to strive for absolute Health.

And, don't forget that we all have the same waters in our bodies, although we all have varying levels of purity and contamination. The quality of our waters — how pure or polluted — is primarily based on what we eat and drink, how often and how much we eat and drink, what and how well we breathe, what we allow to be injected into our blood streams (via vaccines/immunizations), how and how frequently we move the limbs of our bodies, how often and how long we expose ourselves to direct sunlight, how we rest and rejuvenate, and how we think. We want to un-pollute our waters in order to purify the quality of our waters, giving ourselves the best opportunity to see what our Fountains of Youth are capable of. To do so we must identify and remove the lies we've been fed all our lives regarding Health, and we must correct our own minds, as indicated by Lao Tzu, which Patañjali's Yoga Sūtras succinctly explain.

In the next section are some earthly things we can do to show our deep commitment to Health (with a capital "H"), remembering that HEALTH means WHOLE, which is what YOGA is all about — making whole, or joining together into one; atonement (AT-ONE-MENT, "-ment" from Latin mentalis meaning "of the mind").

♦ 9 DIVINE SUGGESTIONS ♦

Following are the nine divine suggestions on where to begin for The Fountain.

1 EAT RIGHT
The guidelines for eating right answer three questions: When to eat, what to eat, and how much to eat?

When to eat? EAT ONLY WHEN HUNGRY
There is an innate intelligence in our bodies that gives us a sure signal when we are hungry and are ready to digest food. It's important that we learn to distinguish "being hungry" from "having an appetite" and honor hunger over appetite. Appetite and hunger are two different things. Hunger is innate intelligence. Appetite is conditioned, trained, and programmed behavior.

KEY: Contrary to popular belief, it is better for Health to NOT eat when hungry than it is to eat when not hungry.

What to eat? EAT ONLY WHAT'S MEANT TO BE EATEN
If you were the first person on the planet, without an instruction manual, what do you think you'd eat? What would catch your attention and draw you to it to eat? A bull might catch your attention, but do you think you'd be drawn in to butcher it and eat it? You'd probably run instead. What about a colorful, succulent looking fruit dangling from a tree across a lush, grassy pasture? That might capture your eye and lure you in. When you approach the fruit, the fragrance might cause you to salivate. And when you bite into the sweet fruit, you might find that your raw, unadulterated senses led you right. As they say, "the nose knows." Why do you think we call the nose "the nose"? Nose and knows are homonyms, and this is by no accident. On the other hand, I doubt slaughtering a cow and seeing all of that blood and tissue would make you salivate. The smell of raw flesh and guts of a bull,

chicken, deer, etc. would not make your mouth water, and might instead make you nauseous and vomit — again, the nose knows!

KEY: Eat light foods. I call plants and plant based produce light foods, because plants perform photosynthesis whereby sunlight is converted into clean, edible energy for humans. Eating this way keeps a person light (as in "not heavy"), keeps a person light on their feet (as in "full of energy"), and promotes brain health for the attainment of light (which is figuratively known as knowledge and wisdom).

A couple favorite resources (books) in this area are:
- The Live Food Factor by Susan Schenck
- Green for Life by Victoria Boutenko

How much to eat? EAT ONLY ENOUGH (to no longer be hungry)
Think about a washing machine. If you stuff so many clothes into it that you can barely close the door on the washer, there will not be enough space for the soap and water to slosh around and clean the clothes. The washer might even struggle to spin optimally. Well, in overly simple terms, the stomach is faced with a similar problem, in that it needs space to slosh so the food can get thoroughly saturated by the digestive juices. When you overeat, you prevent your digestive system from optimally doing what it is designed to do. Overeating also causes fermentation in the gut and leads to undigested food stuff being released into the bloodstream, which pollutes our waters, working against The Fountain.

KEY: Fix smaller portions during meal times and chew your food so thoroughly that you are drinking it by the time you swallow.

2 BREATHE ON PURPOSE
Air is a nutrient we can go the least amount of time without. See how long you can hold your breath to see how vital breathing in air is. Deep breathing takes lots of air into the lungs and oxygenates the blood thereby increasing oxygen in the body and brain. For an idea of just how important oxygen is to an optimally functioning body, here are some symptoms a person might experience when

the blood is deficient in oxygen: fatigue, irritability, digestive issues, depression, confusion, brain fog, a weak immune system, lack of focus, restlessness, etc. A regular practice of deep breathing and breath regulation has the power to counter these and other effects of low oxygen in the body.

The second half of Patañjali's Yoga Sūtras Chapter 2 covers aṣṭaṅga yoga. Aṣṭaṅga is aṣṭau "eight" + aṅga "limbs/parts" so aṣṭaṅga yoga literally means "yoga's eight limbs or parts." The fourth limb, called prāṇāyāma, involves extending and retaining the breath according to certain ratios (or not), as a regular exercise regimen, showing the significance and importance of such a breathing practice. This is ancient knowledge! [See Appendix D for some of the benefits of deep breathing that modern science is beginning to acknowledge, and for a simple, yet effective, breathing practice. See Appendix I for a brief description of all 8 limbs.]

A favorite resource in this area:
- o   Science of Breath by Yogi Ramacharaka.

3 DETOX
What do you think will happen if you get pulled over by the police for driving while "intoxicated"? You might get fined heavily because your judgement and perception, being impaired, puts lives in danger, especially your own, as long as you are behind the wheel. Wait, intoxication affects judgement and perception, and put lives at risk, especially your own? Hmmm... no wonder so many people misjudge the seriousness of this subject (Health) and have impaired perceptions (or no perception at all) regarding actual human health threats, and no wonder so many of us fail to see why it's so important to protect the purity and sanctity of our blood at all cost — they are under the influence and driving their bodies through Life while intoxicated.

Most of us are considerably toxified (aka intoxicated, meaning our bodies are overburdened with toxins) from the foods we eat, beverages we drink (including bottled and fluoridated tap water), and the vaccinations/immunizations we receive (not to mention the deodorants and perfumes/colognes we wear, the soaps and lotions we use, and the air fresheners – really fragrant aerosols – we breathe, etc.), and this intoxication has been so steady and consistent over such a long period of time (often since birth, and even before that due to the intoxication of our mothers who carried us in the womb for nine months), that we've acclimated to this perceptive state of mind and level of consciousness, believing it to be "normal" and "just the way it is," never learning what it feels like to be truly sober until we detox and "experience it" for ourselves. Scratch that, we've not acclimated to this intoxicated state of mind, this is all we've ever known, which is why it's impossible to see beyond it until we've thoroughly detoxed and experienced what it feels like to be clean (at least considerably cleaner than ever before) on a deep cellular level. Once we catch a glimpse and experience a taste of True Health, we're never able to go back to the way it was before.

We must clean our bodies/TEMPLES and keep them clean. To detoxify means to get rid of the toxins in our bodies, and literally "sober up" (saber in Spanish means "to know" and if you're intoxicated, you're not sober, which means "tu no sabes" — or "you don't know" because you're "under the influence"). Although the word toxin and the idea behind it might sound bad enough (if you know toxins are TOXIC contaminants), toxin is actually a euphemism for "poison." Toxins are poisons, and because we consume so many artificial foods these days — foods not grown in gardens or that have been grown in chemical laden, gene-altered gardens — most of us are walking around with toxic, poisoned bodies. Our bodies have become toxic waste dumps, and this is all that many of us can remember, so again, it's normal. (No wonder all the zombie shows over the last decade.)

If you look around, you will bear witness to a drastic weight gain of the population over the past 50 or so years, and an explosion of diseases (in the realms of physical health, mental health, and spiritual health). All the while people are running around confused or clueless as to what's going on and why obesity and disease is at an all time high. Widespread societal ignorance is the effect and consequence of sin saber (Spanish for "not knowing") or simply NOT BEING SOBER.

The best and smartest thing anyone can do to sober up is cleanse/detox and work on purifying their blood and keeping it clean (by eating right and following up with the other suggestions listed with these 9 divine earthly things we can do). Optimum health is contingent on clean, uncontaminated, and pollutant-free blood.

Find a health expert you come to know and trust to learn about a reputable and effective detoxification program/regimen. The word EXPERT in "health expert" implies "experience," meaning that the person you are working with should have experience in healing themselves, which is the only way to know ("have knowledge"). Most medical doctors lack "experience" in this area and are only licensed practitioners (meaning they "practice" on people) with years of rigorous indoctrination (we call "education"), they are NOT experts necessarily! Not to mention that doctors who have never detoxed are just as intoxicated and under the influence as anyone else who has never detoxed, and they are unfit to drive decisions regarding anyone else's health. Your Health is YOUR responsibility, and no one else's, so sober up and gain your own experience to become the only expert to whom you need to listen.

Some favorite resources in this area are:
- Cleanse and Purify Thyself by Dr. Richard Anderson
- www.thedoctorwithin.com with Dr. Tim O'Shea
- Optimum Health Mindset by Yours Truly
- Also, see Appendix E.

4 MOVE YOUR BODY

One of the most important aspects of physical exercise is that you are moving your body. This is because there's another circulatory system in your body besides your blood system, it's called the lymphatic system. Your lymphatic system is largely responsible for helping your body eliminate toxins. The challenge is that, unlike the blood circulatory system, the lymphatic system doesn't have an organ like the heart that's working 24/7 to pump lymph through. The lymphatic system relies on muscular movement and contraction, which is NOT always in action (like the heart), but easily accomplished through physical activity (and even laughing, believe it or not). Walk, dance, jump rope, get on an elliptical, join a Zumba or Jazzercise class, do yoga on-the-mat (the 3rd limb of aṣṭaṅga, which is āsana), practice Tai Chi, play racquetball, whatever, just move your body on a regular basis and get that lymph going. It's called RE-CREATION for a reason.

5 ABSORB DIRECT SUNLIGHT

Like air, sunlight is a nutrient. As often as possible, we want to get plenty of direct sunlight on as much of our bodies as possible (without getting cited for indecent exposure, of course). The use of "sun block" blocks the Sun. We do NOT want to BLOCK the Sun. The Sun is vitally important. Just imagine what would happen if the Sun suddenly ceased to exist. Life would likewise cease to exist. We need the Sun, and we want the Sun to penetrate our bodies, despite what the sellers of these lotions and products say. The sellers of these products are trying to make money, lots and lots of money, so what do we expect them to say? Further, these corporations have deep pockets so don't be surprised that the medical establishment and governments (which are also business enterprises) support this disinformation. No wonder we are educated to fear melanomas and harmful UV rays. And don't be surprised if you learn one day that a company selling sunblock, which actually has been found to contribute to skin cancer, also deals in medical and pharmaceutical sales to treat disease (a clear conflict of interest that's impossible to see if you believe sunblock is healthy and you're under the influence).

Sunlight is a Vitamin! One commonly cited benefit of the Sun is that the human body naturally produces its own Vitamin D when directly exposed to the Sun's rays. No wonder sunblock lotions have been shown to contribute to skin cancers — they interfere with our natural production of Vitamin D, and Vitamin D deficiency is associated with a long list of health problems. What is not mentioned, is that Vitamin D is just one nutritional benefit of direct sunlight exposure that popular science admits (probably because it has been able to isolate it, reproduce it, market it, and sell it), yet there are potentially (rather likely, or undoubtedly if I'm the judge) a plethora more sunlight vitamins not yet identified and/or isolated, and therefore unable to be marketed and sold, which may be why the public hasn't heard of them — more omission. Might it be that if it can't be sold, it won't be told?

What we do know is that vitamin D deficiency contributes to a host of diseases, like: heart disease, osteoporosis, prostate cancer, dementia, erectile dysfunction (in men), schizophrenia, type 2 diabetes, depression, and irritable bowel syndrome (IBS). Other symptoms associated with low vitamin D are fatigue, digestive issues, elevated blood pressure, constipation, restlessness, weight gain, headaches, poor concentration, tooth decay, respiratory infections, and more. And it happens that all of these diseases and symptoms are the source of much profit in the medical and pharmaceutical industries, so there's no incentive to admit the cure; the BIG money is in the treatment. To add, ever wonder why the incidence of colds, flus, and other illnesses goes up in the colder months? We get less Sun. The point here is to GET MORE SUN!

WORD OF CAUTION (especially for people of lighter complexions): Be smart after being indoors for months due to cold weather and being "blocked from the Sun" as a result of wearing clothes to keep warm. Slowly acclimate to direct sunlight exposure so as not to get sunburned (like burnt toast). Perhaps go outside in the sun for 5 minutes one day, 10 minutes the next, 15 the next, and so forth, so as not to go too fast and overdo it in the beginning. Remember, patience is a virtue.

6 THINK RIGHT

Remember KJV Matthew 10:16 from the beginning of Part 1 of this book? "Behold, I send you forth as sheep in the midst of wolves: be ye therefore wise as serpents, and harmless as doves." Thinking right means to be wise, even as serpents, and this requires us to be vigilant at all times, especially when it regards our Health.

One concept many are familiar with that shows the power of the mind, is the matter of placebo. A placebo is often a non-pharmacological substance (usually a simple sugar pill) given to a patient who believes it to be medicine, and simply because it's believed to be a healing agent, disease symptoms reduce or disappear, which is known as the placebo effect. On the flip side, hypochondriacs use the power of belief, which is all mental, to unconsciously manifest disease symptoms. These two examples show the power of the mind in its ability to either allow healing or to produce dis-ease. The mind is more powerful than most of us can imagine!

The placebo effect shows what happens when the mind fully believes in a thing, where to "believe fully" is also known as having "complete and utter faith." When we have complete and utter faith in something, then we have NO doubt that it will happen according to its promise, and we therefore don't worry because there is absolutely no reason to worry. The relinquishment of worry is a crucial element when it comes to thinking right because "to worry" means to cause "war" in the mind (creating mental dis-ease), and therefore the body (creating physical dis-ease), which interferes with health (being whole).

Not only can we hear the word war in the first syllable of worry, an investigation into the word origins and meanings of these words reveals how they're linked. One of the meanings of worry is "to vex, harass." To harass means "to harry," to harry means "to make war," and war means "to confuse, to bring into a state of confusion." When we take the necessary actions to become un-confused, by thinking, learning, and retraining ourselves to do right, and we take impeccable care of our bodies, it's easier to NOT worry. When we acquiesce to a state of confusion and don't take deliberate care of our physical health, deep within we know we are not doing right by the body, and are therefore prone to reach a point of worry at some point in time, which is fear-based. So, treat your body like the temple it is at all times, and relinquish any doubt that you are completely healthy.

In Patañjali's Yoga Sūtra 1.23, not only are we given a key for attaining a state of yoga, we are also given the secret on how to NOT worry, keeping in mind that we must live in congruence with that which we have complete and utter faith in. This sūtra reads Īśvara - praṇidhānādvā where Īśvara means "the infinitely intelligent divine ideal of pure awareness" and praṇidhānād means "complete and total self-surrender and submission." This Awareness, being infinitely intelligent and ALL-KNOWING, knows exactly what we all need, knows what we all need to do, and knows how to speak to us at just the right time to let us know what we need and need to do when we are prepared and ready to listen and do it.

Think about it, if this Divine Awareness is all-knowing, how can its Voice (which may show up as a sign, insight, creative idea, whatever) ever steer anyone wrong? Being ALL-knowing, it can't make a mistake or steer us wrong, we just have to learn to hear it and Trust it. Try this: Even when things don't seem to be going your way, assume that this infinitely intelligent divine ideal of pure awareness (whether you call it God, The Universe, The Oversoul, Allah, or whatever) is conspiring to pull strings in your favor to help you win in the end. Always look for the silver lining, it's there. Just remember, you are still alive and you are a work in progress. It takes time to make a masterpiece, which YOU ARE in the making — we all are.

Further, with regard to thinking right, keep in mind that CSF is practically nothing but water. If you've come across the work of the Japanese scientist, Dr. Masaru Emoto (a couple of his books are The Secret Life of Water and Love Thyself: The Message from Water), then you are probably aware of the claims of his scientific findings. He put words on glasses of water, then through a technique that allows water to be frozen for observation, he found that different words had different effects on the crystalline structure of the water. For instance, water contained in a glass with the word LOVE on it, was observed to have a crystalline structure that was symmetrical; while, on the other hand, the crystalline structure of water contained in a glass that had the word HATE on it, was asymmetrical and distorted. In his experiments, symmetry represents beauty and the lack of symmetry, or distortion, represents ugliness. The question is: If words on a glass have this effect on the water contained within it, what effect do we think our thoughts have on us, being that our bodies are containers holding our own vital waters?

Consistent with Emoto's findings, we are informed by Patañjali's Yoga Sūtra 1.33 to dwell upon thoughts of friendliness, compassion, and delight, regardless of whether we are happy or unhappy, and despite whether we construe circumstances or people as good or bad. This sūtra goes on to state that by doing so, a calm and tranquil mind will be cultivated. Then, in sūtra 2.33, we are told to dwell upon thoughts and ideas of a salubrious nature for auspicious results, as unrefined and unwholesome thoughts lead to reckless and injurious actions which invariably produce inauspicious results. (See Appendix F for the transliterations of these sūtras, the word-for-word meanings, and an overall translation of each).

Anyone interested in correcting her or his mind is encouraged to learn, study, and apply the practical wisdom of Patañjali's Yoga Sūtras (which I happen to teach online and at yoga studios). This is emphasized and revisited in greater depth and detail at the end of this list of nine divine suggestions — #9 PRACTICE YOGA. [FYI: In my courses, students learn how to chant the sūtras in their original Sanskrit, their word-for-word meanings, and their overall translations (so they don't have to rely on someone else to interpret the sūtras for them). To view upcoming courses and online workshops OR for collaboration opportunities, please visit damongivehand.com to learn more.]

Some favorite resources in this area:
- o The Secret Life of Water by Masaru Emoto
- o The Biology of Belief by Bruce Lipton
- o Any translation of Patañjali's Yoga Sūtras will do that you can find that resonates with you. I suggest a few at my website, and here is one many of my students have expressed appreciation for... The Yoga Sutras of Patanjali by Swami Satchidananda

7 SLEEP AND GET ADEQUATE REST
When we sleep, this is when the body has a chance to repair, replenish, revitalize, and rejuvenate. Our bodies do this automatically as long as we allow it and do NOT interfere with it. Another way to think of it is that this is the time the infinitely intelligent divine ideal of pure awareness gets to work on the body without interference, so we want to give it adequate, uninterrupted time to do its thing! Quality sleep is far too undeRESTimated!

The trouble is that many of us remain so busy much of the time, filling every nook and cranny of our days and weeks with activities that ultimately diminish the quality of our sleep and reduce the amount of time we have to sleep, given our commitments and obligations, that our health silently suffers because it doesn't get the time it needs to repair, replenish, revitalize, and rejuvenate like it's designed to.

TIP: Make the conscious decision to put "adequate quality sleep" at or near the top of your list of priorities, and ruthlessly nix those activities that really aren't that important or necessary and only get in the way of sound sleep. See APPENDIX G for a few Adequate Quality Rest recommendations.

8 FAST

Fasting simply means "not eating" and it's good to "not eat" at certain times, and for extended periods from time to time. We eat as much as we do because we have literally been trained to eat as much as we do. There is no other natural species on the planet that (in its natural habitat) eats when it's not hungry or eats a routine 3 meals per day with light snacks in between, not to mention that "junk food" doesn't exist at all in a "natural" habitat.

We believe we are supposed to have 3 square meals a day, and this kind of thinking leads people to eat even when they are not hungry. Commercial ads and marketers have been bombarding us our entire lives, from the time we are in the womb until we are dead, with clever language and images to get us to override our natural innate intelligence to eat whatever we want whenever we want (unaware that what we want has often been manipulated and influenced by ads, marketing methods, and education).

When we eat even though we are not hungry, we are putting food down the hatch before the hatch is clear at the bottom. Imagine if a bathtub takes in water faster than it drains, what will happen? The tub will fill up and overflow. Eventually, if we continually outpace our elimination, our systems will likewise back up. When the body's system gets clogged or backed up, we call this "congestion" which literally means the opposite of digestion when you observe the etymology of each of these terms.

When our internal plumbing is clogged, our internal sewage system tries to find other ways of removing sewage from the body (snot, sneezing, phlegm, coughing, diarrhea, etc.). The body even sends a strong message to the sick person causing them to lose their appetites or to vomit when they do try to eat before the body is ready, causing us to fast involuntarily. Along with eating right, keep your body unclogged/uncongested and never worry about getting sick again. (see APPENDIX C)

A favorite resource in this area:
- o The Master Cleanser by Stanley Burroughs

9 PRACTICE YOGA

Up to this point in my journey, the single most obvious thing that all roads lead to for "how to" develop and access the extraordinary powers of our fountains of youth is undoubtedly Yoga (or "geoghah"), as it's described and explained in Patañjali's Yoga Sūtras. The Yoga Sūtras of Patañjali represent the authoritative text on Yoga, explicitly explaining what Yoga is, why it's necessary, and how to practice it, among other things.

It's a dead giveaway that the wisdom contained in Patañjali's Yoga Sūtras has directly to do with the Fountain of Youth because of the expression Patañjali's Yoga itself. Observe that Patañjali is a compound of Ptah (listen) and añjali, Ptah being "opener" or "mouth (of a river)" and añjali meaning "divine offering." In Old English, at least as far back as c.1200 (but probably earlier), the word mouth conveyed an "outfall of a river" and the word river meant "a copious flow (of water)" just as it means today; so a mouth was an "outfall of a copious flow (of water)." Meanwhile, the word fountain is a combination of the Latin fons "spring (of water)" plus the PIE root dhen- "to run, flow," making the words mouth, which is symbolized by Ptah, and fountain practically synonymous and interchangeable (especially recalling from earlier that spring means "source of a stream, river, or flow of water").

Then, when considering that añjali means "divine offering," and the word offer (as in divine OFFERing) comes from ob "to, toward, against, across" + ferre (from PIE bher-) "to bring, to carry, to bear children," we see the easy connection it shares with the EWE-TAURUS of the brain (uterus being "the bearer of children"), aka the ventricular ("little belly") system containing the choroid plexuses which neuro-anatomists and scientists acknowledge as the point of origin for CSF (the special amniotic water of this divine fountain). Recall also that choroid means "outer membrane of a fetus sac," implying an inner membrane (amnion) within which fetuses are conceived and developed in a swell of cerebrospinal amniotic fluid (whose accomplishment is represented by ewe + th = youth) before they are born or "offered," as indicated by añjali.

Furthermore, as we've also already addressed, the root of the word yoga is Sanskrit yuj or PIE yeug, and the roots of those roots are yu and yeu, respectively. The practice of yoga is the process of cultivating, developing, and refining "vital force" (yu/yeu) so that we may become whole again (at which point we may be liberated from our shortcomings). Earlier we covered how the -th suffix of a word signifies the accomplishment of the notion of the base, which in the case of youth (you+th, yeu/yu+th, or ewe+th) is you (aka yu/yeu or ewe). So, the word youth conveys the accomplishment of the notion of yu/yeu, which means the accomplishment of the notion of vital force which is the central focus of the practice of yoga; it also signifies the accomplishment of that which develops in ewe (and eye), which is the chief and foremost "vital fluid" — the divine amniotic CSF.

In light of the foregoing, given what we've shown Ptah, añjali, and yoga to mean and what these have to do with, Patañjali's Yoga Sūtras could just as appropriately be called The Fountain of Youth's Sūtras. Therefore, learning, studying, exemplifying, and embodying what Patañjali's Yoga Sūtras teach is a clear and necessary fundamental step for developing and accessing the powers of our fountains, and of the utmost importance to the earnest Student of Life (S.O.L.) who's genuinely interested in exploring this new and exciting unknown frontier. (And remember that YOGA and The BIBLE fit like hand-in-glove and The Bible is about The Fountain.)

There is most certainly more to figure out and know than just the practical wisdom of Patañjali's Yoga Sūtras, but there is no doubt that this is an essential piece of the puzzle and therefore there is no better place to start. To begin learning Patañjali's Yoga Sūtras, you can pick up any one of a good number of translations from a list of reliable and trustworthy contemporary authors (you can visit my website for a list). However, please remember that when you rely solely on understanding what Patañjali's Yoga Sūtras mean based on the words of a single author, you are limiting your own understanding to the limits of the interpreter you are learning from. For this reason, I recommend picking up a translation (or two or three) to read that resonates with you, while also learning the word-for-word meanings of the transliterated sūtras from their original Sanskrit so that you can see where the author you're reading may be coming from (based on the examples they share, the stories they tell, and the context they provide), and so you can eventually explain what the sūtras mean in your own words. I also sincerely recommend learning to chant the sūtras so that the practical wisdom contained in the text gets ingrained in you on a cellular level and absorbed on every level allowing you to become one with the book constantly and continuously shining its light while unconsciously giving others permission to do the same (like Marianne Williamson lets us know in her poem Our Greatest Fear).

To palpably and authentically learn Patañjali's Yoga Sūtras in a genuine way — I'm talking about the word-for-word meanings and how to chant the sūtras in their original Sanskrit — I've created a space where you can learn this deep wisdom with other like-minded individuals whose curiosities are as piqued as yours. To learn more, visit damongivehand.com.

♦ FINAL WORDS (for now) ♦

We've shown the amniotic CSF to be the water of this Fountain, and the choroid plexuses of the ventricular system to be The Fountain from which this special water springs and flows forth (recalling that ventricle literally means "little belly" and is part of what forms what we now recognize as the EWE-TAURUS of the brain), which gives new perspective on the concept of rebirth and the realm of possibility regarding what it means to be reborn. In light of this new knowledge, being reborn is more than a figurative idea of taking on a new attitude in life, as there is obviously a real womb in the brain whose purpose and function must be to undergo a real pregnancy, by way of an IMMACULATE CONCEPTION, given the right acts and conditions (just like the kind of pregnancy we're all familiar with that takes place in the lower reproductive region of the woman or womb-man — the right acts and conditions must be had).

So, when it's all said and done, this book has been about identifying the TRUE MATRIX, as matrix means "uterus, womb." Who knew there is a literal womb inside our skulls in our brains? Like the movie (The Matrix) says… the reality we've been coaxed into seeing everywhere we look and into believing exists all around us is a "world that has been pulled over (our) eyes to blind (us) from the truth" (~Morpheus). To know this heavenly Truth (funny how the word know has sexual connotations when we listen to the written dialogues of older times, keeping in mind that sex is a prerequisite to pregnancy), we must be willing to traverse and travail the strait gate and narrow way mentioned in (KJV) Matthew 7:14 that few find (which means few "obtain by search or study" and can also be interpreted as there are few who will find the path itself AS WELL AS the spiritual courage, moral strength, and divine patience we must muster to eagerly and enthusiastically sustain such an odyssey), as this is the way that leadeth unto life or re-birth (whatever this actually and truly means — which is most probably unlike anything we can imagine given that the current world structure goes to such great lengths to confuse us and obscure this Great Truth, whether unintentionally or intentionally).

Indeed, where do we go from here? I grew up loving the series Star Trek, yet it turns out they were far from the final frontier. Playing off a 1968 episode of Star Trek that was humorously redone on the sitcom In Living Color — We must be out of our Vulcan minds! The Fountain of Youth is wide open for exploration and discovery, and I hope you'll join me in the quest of this new and fresh frontier (it's new and fresh to us anyway, because we know there's really nothing new under the Sun).

Hope you enjoyed this and find the content contained herein and this topic to be interesting, refreshing, important, inspirational, and of immense, practical value, touching on some things you may not have encountered, considered, or thought of before. In a world that wishes to convince us there is nothing else to learn because it's all already been figured out, let this work serve as evidence to the contrary — THERE IS SO MUCH MORE TO LEARN THAN WE'VE EVER IMAGINED, and now's the time!

If you wish to be part of a growing community of curious explorers in this area, and would like to receive updates as we learn and discover more in this direction (all things related to the Fountain of Youth Truth), AND if you wish to learn Patañjali's Yoga Sūtras with me, visit my website to learn more. I guarantee no one else is teaching Patañjali's Yoga Sūtras in a way that considers a Fountain of Youth context, at least YET anyway. Now the door has been opened. Along with me, be among the first to enter. We are far from the final frontier!

(KJV) ST. JOHN 4:14
But whosoever drinketh of the water that I shall give him shall never thirst; but the water that I shall give him shall be in him a well of water springing up into everlasting life.

Just remember, we are not even scratching the surface of the scratch that scratches the surface, and there is so much more I deliberately did not go into or mention. Be on the lookout for the forthcoming edited, polished, and glossy version. To be among the first to know of its release, as well as other books specifically related to this subject matter, join my Inner Circle (at damongivehand.com) to receive my monthly newsletter where I'll share the latest discoveries and epiphanies, release fresh content you can find nowhere else, offer resources and free giveaways, mention new book releases (which are all directly or indirectly connected), and announce upcoming classes/courses, retreats, and other events. Also, if interested in exploring possible collaboration opportunities contact me at damongivehand.com/contact.html. I love doing interviews, writing articles, and contributing guest blog posts to get the word out, so if you or anyone you know is interested in any of these, that's the best way to contact me.

Thank YOU for reading!!! I sincerely hope you found much philosophical and practical value in this work! PLEASE REVIEW THIS BOOK sharing your honest feedback, and feel free to contact me with questions, comments, and other connections relevant to this content. Since much of the work I do and the perspective I bring is often new, I consider this a conversation and welcome input from anyone sincerely interested in getting to the pure, unadulterated, wholesome Truth. Don't make the mistake of discounting anything covered, let me know if there is anything I can clear up or elaborate on to bring better understanding. Hearing what you have to say and the questions you ask helps me zero in and focus on what else needs to be considered, what needs to be clarified, and where to dig deeper.

Shalom, Shanti, Peace, Hotep, Namaste...
~Damon

Throughout this book (the appendices excluded), the intent has been to present content that is irrefutable based on your ability to see, hear, and make proper connections among and between ideas and your own experience(s). In the appendices I introduce pieces that may seem refutable if you haven't experienced these before, however, if you've practiced these then your personal experience (pratyaksha) will provide all the proof you need.

Damon Givehand

APPENDIX A — GETTING QUIET SO WE CAN HEAR WHEN WE LISTEN

To get QUIET in order to hear better: Sit tall wherever you can find a comfortable seat, whether cross legged or in a chair with your feet flat on the floor; gently pull your shoulders back opening your rib cage, and slightly tuck your chin; then, take several deep breaths in through the nose completely filling your chest first and then the belly before exhaling back through the nose twice as long as your inhale (for instance, if you inhale for a count of 4, then exhale for a count of 8; if you inhale for 5 or 6, then exhale for 10 or 12, respectively). DO THIS for at least 8-10 breath cycles, remembering to focus on the breath while comfortably lengthening your spine with each inhale as you sit and breathe TO QUIET YOURSELF. (If your mind is not relatively quiet after 8-10 of these breaths, continue this pattern of breathing for 10-15 minutes more, or longer if you like. Quieting the mind takes practice because it's not something most of us are used to. So be patient with yourself and know that you will develop this skill over time as long as you remain committed to a regular breathing practice. Persistent consistency is the price of admission for EVERYONE, no exceptions. For anyone not willing to pay the price, entrance will not be granted).

LISTEN

Don't skip the step on first becoming quiet. Getting quiet is a crucial step in listening to figure out new things and connect new dots that degreed scholars and other authors/researchers may not have connected yet. Remember, you don't have to wait for them to catch up with the WHOLE TRUTH! Let them work on their truths based on their own unique curiosities at their pace while YOU DO YOU. Sometimes listening means literally listening to the phonetic sound of a word so that the obvious may reveal itself, and other times it's listening with your eye of understanding to the root meanings of words that cause lights of insight (in+sight or "sight that's inside") to suddenly activate.

Damon Givehand

APPENDIX B — HOW TO READ THE BIBLE

(KJV) MATTHEW 13:34
ALL these things spake Jesus unto the multitude in parables; and without a parable spake he not unto them.

All ancient texts are valuable, however, the King James Version (KJV) Bible happens to be best for the context of this book. All stories of ancient religions are deeply connected with the zodiac, and that is where individuals of those faiths are recommended to place their efforts in peeling back the layers in search of Truth with a capital "T" if the Truth is what they're really after. All pieces of the Truth puzzle fit together, so when we are reading whatever ancient religious book correctly, they all syncretize seamlessly. Truth is not an institutional religion, and Truth doesn't rely on emotions; TRUTH JUST IS. When reading the Bible, there are a couple key things to ALWAYS keep in mind that might help in comprehending the profound message contained in the Bible (especially as it pertains to the Fountain of Youth):

1. You have to use your WHOLE BRAIN to properly and accurately interpret it. When people think the Bible is one dimensional and only represents a literal account of the past, and they expend their efforts in arguing and trying to prove the existence of this person or that (especially Jesus as a historical character), that is the left logical brain (and I use "left" here to denote sinister and rational, not left-hand side) that sees differences and how things are apart, disconnected, separate, and NOT related. The left brain is also the "low" brain. The right brain (i.e. the "correct" brain or "high" brain), which some refer to as the creative, spiritual brain, sees similarities and how things are alike, connected, the same, and related. The whole brain, which is ruled by the right brain, considers what's logical while seeking to figure out how EVERYTHING RELATES, so it can see the WHOLE PICTURE, thus the word HOLY (or WHOLLY, an adverb). Anyone who is dominated by logic alone is LEFT brain driven, and the word left actually means "sinister" (look it up), while right means "not wrong" or "correct" or "upright" like 90 degrees (and the word wright means "work" so correct seeing is not something that happens passively).

2. ALL of the teachings of Jesus are given in parable — not some, ALL (see the verse above from the Bible itself that states it) — so we must ALWAYS go beyond the surface of what the verses "appear" to mean and go deeper to find True meaning. The Bible is NOT one dimensional, and was NOT written by a one-dimensional people — our GGs were highly advanced and their brain development was reflective of a Golden Age.

APPENDIX C — FASTING

What I do now to protect the sanctity of my blood and maintain a clean body...

Nowadays, I do a 10-day to two-week fast seasonally, I do a one-day fast weekly, AND I fast for at least 3 consecutive days each month when the moon is transiting my sun sign. I don't eat meat or artificial foods. I eat mostly raw, organic produce (especially green plants), I consume soup broths, I drink lots of herbal teas and fresh juice (love that chlorophyll!), and I'm satisfied on about a meal and a half per day. When people say they can't afford to eat healthy, it's usually because they eat too often (and they're trying to find "organic" alternatives to replace old vices, and those products being marketed as organic are often considerably more pricey). If you keep to eating simple and clean, you actually spend a lot less on food, plus you stay healthy and never have to spend money on medications that sick people feel the need to spend money on.

Kiala and I spend less on food now than we ever did on the Standard American Diet (SAD). It took me some years to evolve to this point though, because there was a time when "eating healthy" did break my bank (they don't call Whole Foods "whole paycheck" for nothin'), but that was when I was trying to find organic replacements of my old conventional vices while maintaining a pace of at least 3 meals per day. That is when I thought I knew what "eating healthy" meant, but based on what I know now I was still way off the mark (even though I was feeling better than I ever did before my first cleanse).

Fast (weekly, monthly, seasonally, and intermittently — we don't need as much food as we've been programmed to believe we do). If you have not fasted as a practice before, then this may not be an area where you are able to realize the truth upon "hearing" it, because you lack the actual experience necessary to remember. If, on the other hand, you have fasted "as a practice" before (not once or twice for a day, a weekend, or a week, but as a regular practice over time), then you are more likely to resonate with the soundness of fasting as an integral part of your perpetual life.

First, recognize that usually when the word FAST is encountered, it has to do with the speed, swiftness, or rapidity of a thing. Another word often used synonymously with fast is quick (which unbeknownst by many means "living, lively, alive, ready, sprightly, full of life" from PIE gwei- "to live"). To quicken means "to come to life" or "give life to." Recall that life has to do with possessing "vital force" (yeu-, the root of yuj which is the root of yoga), so when something quickens, its vital force is either activated or augmented. Anyone who fasts regularly can attest to this. If you've never fasted before, the only way you will ever know of the quickening effect of fasting is to test it. If you do wish to fast, you are recommended to consult with a trusted and experienced guide or friend on how best to approach fasting. Fasting is like electricity, you should not fear it, but you must respect it or it will knock you on your tail. Near the end of this appendix, I share a glimpse of my fasting practice (but again, find someone you know and trust to guide you through this and who will support you along the way). Before that though, following are some more thoughts related to the notion of fasting.

Remember that, as a "civilized" society, we eat more than any other species on the planet. No other life form in its natural habitat eats three or more meals a day, not to mention snacks interspersed throughout — all natural life forms eat when they're hungry. We eat when we feel like it, whether hungry or not, and we think we feel like it more than the body can keep up with. When you add in the fact that we also consume lots of foods that are not food at all (like toxic mystery ingredients, GMO's, etc.), we further compound the problem of eating. Considering the fact that we eat so much (and so much of the wrong things), and the incidence of disease is steadily climbing with no plateau in sight, it only makes sense that we give the body a rest from time to time, so it doesn't have to breakdown and synthesize all the food and nonfood we constantly bombard our digestive systems with.

Even in ancient times, long before the modern fake food industry spawned, fasting ("voluntarily abstaining from consuming food or drink") was recognized in practically all ancient religions. The word religion is actually re- "again, back" + ligion "to bind" (from Latin ligare), and to bind is to "fasten." Notice the word fast in FASTen, which means "to bind." The word fast also carries with it another meaning ("speedily") similar to a meaning quick carries ("rapid"), both conveying a notion of swiftness, and this is how the two words, fast and quick, are linked. Quick also means "alive, full of life, lively, ready" (as an adjective); and, something most probably don't know, as a noun it means "living persons" in contrast to those who are dead. Anyone who fasts regularly and eats a clean diet will tell you that fasting does have a quickening effect (where quicken means "come to life") and makes you feel alive and ready to go.

Those who combine regular fasting with eating right, not only procure slim and slender bodies without excess weight (as nature intended), they generally experience more energy, get better sleep, need less sleep, feel calmer, think clearer, have greater self-control, and emanate an overall agreeable attitude, ALL of which are consistent with coming alive, being full of life, and feeling ready.

There is a reason that gluttony (overeating) is considered a SIN in the Bible. Remember, AS ABOVE, SO BELOW and the Bible (BI+BULL) talks about two BELLies (or Bulls), the one above and the one below (remember the uterus and the ewe-taurus). Over stuffing the lower belly requires the body to concentrate all of its digestive forces in the lower belly. SIN means "to come up short" (as sin in Spanish means "without" signifying that something is missing, and because something is missing we come up short of being complete). If the body is "consumed" with breaking down foods that fill the lower belly, this means the upper belly is not fully attended to, and therefore "comes up short."

MY FASTING REGIMENT
For me, regular fasting consists of fasting intermittently (which is daily), weekly, monthly, and seasonally. What does each of these look like?
Intermittent fasting — No more than two meals a day, but usually a meal and a half. Not eating until around noon and not eating after 6pm or sundown. Roughly speaking, only eating between the hours of noon and 6pm equates to daily fasts of 18 hours.
Weekly fasting — Picking one day per week to NOT eat. While following the intermittent fasting protocol, this turns out to be

about 42 hours (for example: no food after 6pm Sunday, no food all day Monday, and no food until after noon Tuesday)

Monthly fasting — Not eating for three consecutive days each month (equates to about 90 hours)

Seasonal fasting — Each season, not eating for a period of at least 10 days up to 2 weeks (sometimes 3). This is also a time to detox and do a deep cleanse. Do not attempt an extended fast without doing your homework and consulting with a qualified, reliable, and trustworthy person. Fasts should not be feared, but they must be respected. Checkout the short book The Master Cleanser by Stanley Burroughs, if you are looking for more direction and instruction on cleansing fasts.

APPENDIX D — THE POWER OF BREATHING ON PURPOSE

The modern field of psychology is finally recognizing and admitting what the ancients have long known about breathing. Here are some benefits today's research is reporting and attributing to deep, slow breathing...

FEELING CALM AND TRANQUIL — breathing deeply stimulates the parasympathetic nervous system, which is responsible for states of relaxation. So less stress and anxiety.

BETTER POSTURE — breathing deeply encourages the chest to open, rib cage to expand, and the spine to lift and straighten when inhaling, countering the tendency to slouch.

HEALTHIER BLOOD — breathing deeply causes you to take in large amounts of oxygen (which has cleansing and alkalizing properties), and release a good amount of toxins by breathing out. So, inhaling deeply has the effect of cleansing, alkalizing, and oxygenating our bodies, while exhaling deeply detoxifies, working together to help our blood be more pure.

BETTER PAIN MANAGEMENT — breathing deeply causes our brains to release certain endorphins responsible for relieving pain, so pain may be reduced or eliminated by this method.

IMPROVED DIGESTION — the digestive system needs oxygen to function properly. Deep breathing increases oxygen intake thereby making sure an adequate supply of this vital element is present for proper digestion.

LOWERED BLOOD PRESSURE — breathing deeply and slowly causes blood vessels to relax and dilate, bringing blood pressure to proper levels.

GREATER CLARITY — by concentrating attention on deep breathing, not only do we stop focusing on unproductive and/or unconstructive, distracting thoughts for the time by connecting with the present, we also slow our bodies down and become more relaxed. A relaxed mind can see more vividly, is more creative, and more equipped to make sound decisions and see innovative solutions.

AND THE LIST GOES ON...

One powerful practice is alternate nostril breathing...
1. Find a quiet space and sit comfortably.

2. Rest your left hand on your lap, thigh, or knee (palm facing up or down, whatever's most comfortable).

3. Bend the first two fingers (index and middle) of your right hand toward your palm, and gently place your thumb and ring finger on your nose, below the bridge and near top of nostrils (thumb on right nostril / ring finger on left nostril).

4. Spend a few moments in this position breathing gently, just noticing your breath and finger placement.

5. Close your eyes and exhale, then...
    o close your right nostril by softly pressing thumb, leaving left nostril open
    o inhale slowly and deeply through left nostril
    o pause (split second) release right nostril by lifting thumb while closing your left nostril by gently pressing ring finger
    o exhale right nostril slowly and completely
    o pause (split second)
    o inhale right nostril slowly and deeply
    o pause, gently release left nostril, close your right nostril by softly pressing thumb
    o exhale left nostril
    o pause
    o inhale left nostril
    o pause, ALTERNATE NOSTRILS, and repeat this pattern for 3-5 minutes, or longer if desired

Points to remember:
- inhales and exhales should be of equal length/duration (in this sequence); this can be accomplished by mentally counting during breaths
- alternate with slight pauses after inhales and exhales
- finish alternate nostril breathing with an exhale
- when finished with alternate nostril breathing, remain seated and breathe naturally for a minute or two.
- then go have an amazing rest of your day!

This practice can get more advanced, with holds and different breathing ratios, but this is a good and safe starting point.

Alternate nostril breathing is one of the most powerful and effective tools anyone can ever have, especially when overwhelm starts to creep in or when life seems to be spiraling out of control, turning the potential of your Fountain of Youth into a whirlpool. The next time such things might happen, give yourself permission to not be caught in your thoughts, find a quiet place, and do some alternate nostril breathing. When you come back, all will be clearer.

Damon Givehand

APPENDIX E — DETOX, CLEANSE, MAINTAIN

We live in a system where dollars determine what information gets blasted on TV, radio, training programs, public literature, and other media sources. To "publicize" means to make known to the "public" or to advertise. The deepest pockets spend millions and even billions to publicize and advertise information that casts their products or services in a favorable light. Sadly, their reach even extends into "public" education, and modern education has transformed into an agency geared toward shaping what and how people think (which leads to "predictable" behavior). There is no watchdog overseeing these heavy spenders to make sure the information they are spreading and reinforcing is advantageous for its human consumers. You and I have to be our own watchdogs.

One result of dollar driven information is the general public's poor disposition on health. One school of thought, the school with the deep pockets and that spends much to shape public opinion (thinking and behavior), has the general public (majority of society) believing in ideas like: disease is genetic, colds and flus are contagious, cancer is incurable, and that "prescription" drugs help restore health, among many more wrong and flawed notions. This school of thought is also a very new/young school of thought, whose influence increased significantly over the last century, right around the time that rates of disease started to skyrocket, and "disease management" (a more fitting expression than "healthcare") became one of the world's most profitable industries ever (which is why they have so much money to spend on prescription drug propaganda). This school of thought fails to view the human being as a whole organism who is more than the sum of its parts, and therefore attempts to "treat" symptoms (as nebulous as these can be) based on a person's unique biological weakness at the time (whether an organ, tumor location, physiological system, etc.).

There is another school of thought that views the human being as a whole entity (where the whole human being is seen as greater than the sum of her or his parts), and that sets out to heal the whole human being. In this view, there is but one dis-ease instead of many different diseases. One name given to this condition of disease is autointoxication, which simply means the body has been toxified (taken in too many toxins) to a degree that it can no longer function in a state of "ease" (therefore this state is called "dis-ease"). The first approach to healing the whole body is to get all the toxins out of the body, which is called cleansing, detoxing, or detoxifying. This school of thought actually fixes people permanently, and without life-long customers there is very little profit to be made compared to the previous example. [The misnamed healthcare system and the pharmaceutical industry hate this school of thought because it threatens their enormous profits, so they educate people to believe their way is the best way (even their method of education sets out to confuse — just listen to how confused people are about health).] This school of thought is for people ready to assume responsibility for their own health and well-being; the school of thought in the first example is for people who don't want the responsibility of their own health and would rather leave it up to… whoever else.

EDUCATE YOURSELF...
Netflix has a documentary called The Beautiful Truth, where a 15 year old investigates how to cure cancer by way of diet. This is how I was first exposed to Max Gerson's work back in about 2008, and Gerson Therapy. Max has long since passed, but his daughter Charlotte Gerson (96 at the time of this writing) is still alive and kicking, and as sharp and spunky as ever. Gerson Therapy also uses coffee enemas, another powerful detoxifying method when done properly.

There are lots of other documentaries out there that expose a compromised food and medicine system, and we are encouraged to assume responsibility over our own health, which is the mature thing to do. That said, go learn as much as you can with the full knowledge that the human body is designed to be disease-free.

And know this… most people today, and I was NO EXCEPTION to the rule (visit damongivehand.com and read "My Fat Story"), are fat or can't lose that midsection because they eat foods that are not meant to be eaten AND/OR they eat too often (3 times a day plus sporadic snacks in between — that's too much). Eating too much corrupts the blood and therefore the Fountain's water (Mary). If we keep our blood clean, we are good to go.

Also, I didn't mention this in Appendix C, but when I do my longer fasts each season, I also do some deep cleansing with "internal salt water baths" and/or coffee enemas. I didn't mention this until now because of #1 on the following list that lists the Master Cleanser.

A FEW OF MY PREFERRED SEASONAL CLEANSING & MAINTENANCE OPTIONS...
1. Master Cleanser developed by Stanley Burroughs
    o This is essentially a lemonade (with cayenne and maple syrup) fast.
    o By the time of this writing, the longest I've done this cleanse is 24 days, although a 40 day fast is on the horizon.
    o I've always done this cleanse while incorporating what Stanley calls "Internal Salt Water Bathing" (he goes over this in his book).
2. Green juice fasts
    o You may have seen the documentary Fat Sick & Nearly Dead, and now there's a part 2. Last I checked, these were both a "Watch Now" on Netflix, if you happen to have an account with that provider. You can also catch it on Hulu if you have access to that (which was also available at the time of this writing).
3. Enemas and colon hydrotherapy
    o The first time I had my colon irrigated, I did it with a colon hydrotherapist, and the result was amazing. I did it this way first so I could have trusted and reputable guidance in something with which I had no experience.
    o Enemas are at home DIY colon irrigation. I learned the art of self-administering enemas because of the feeling I experienced when having my colon flushed the first time with guidance. The cost of colon hydrotherapy might be a bit of an expense if needing it for a maintenance program. Home enemas cost nothing more than the cost of an enema bucket, tube, and time to learn how to self-administer. This is my preferred method for ongoing life/health maintenance. I also

consider this a major reason I've not gotten sick in the slightest since 2008.

APPENDIX F — 3 KEY SUTRA TRANSLITERATIONS AND TRANSLATIONS

1.23   Īśvara - praṇidhānādvā.

Īśvara = divine ideal of pure awareness; Infinite Intelligence; God; etc.
praṇidhānād = complete and total submission; by self-surrender or resignation to; alignment; dedication;
vā = or; selection; an option.

TRANSLATION: (Yoga may also be achieved) by completely submitting and surrendering to the "divine ideal of pure awareness" (Īśvara).

This sutra is about the cultivation of True Faith (different than blind faith).

1.33   Maitrīkaruṇā - muditopekṣāṇām - sukhaduḥkha - puṇyāpuṇyaviṣayāṇām - bhāvanātaḥ - cittaprasādanam;

maitrī = friendliness;
karuṇā = compassion; mercy;
mudita = delight; gladness; joy;
upekṣāṇām = equanimity; indifference; disregard of;
sukha = happiness; joy;
duḥkha = sorrow; misery; distress; pain; suffering; unhappiness;
puṇya = good; virtuous; virtue;
apuṇya = not good (bad); not virtuous (evil); vice; wicked;
viṣayāṇām = object (of exp); concerning a thing;
bhāvanātaḥ = by dwelling upon in mind; radiating; projecting; by cultivating attitudes;
citta = mind; consciousness;
prasādanam = undisturbed calmness; tranquilizing; purification.

TRANSLATION: The mind becomes calm and tranquil (i.e. devoid of the symptoms accompanying a distracted mind) BY dwelling upon and projecting friendliness (maitrī), compassion (karuṇā), and delight (mudito) toward ALL things whether or not regarded as pleasurable (sukha), pain-producing (duḥkha), good/virtuous (puṇya), or bad/evil (apuṇya). [So do this as a first option.]

Distract = dis "apart, away" + tract "to draw," so a distracted mind is a mind that is drawn apart or away. Yoga draws or joins the mind together, to become whole again, and not a-part.

2.33   vitarkabādhane - pratipakṣabhāvanam
vitarka = (in terms of the kind/quality of thinking) gross, unrefined, analytical, unwholesome
bādhane = harmful hurtful actions, obstructions/obstacles, characterized by disturbance
prati = opposite
pakṣa = side
bhāvanām = attitude, visualization, feeling produced by dwelling upon in mind

TRANSLATION: Analytical thoughts leading one to be disturbed can be undone, reversed, or neutralized by dwelling upon opposite kinds of thoughts.

APPENDIX G — ADEQUATE QUALITY REST

Recommendations are:
- o Get at least 6-8 hours (or however much you require to feel FULLY rejuvenated) of really good, sound, and uninterrupted sleep. Always remember that it's during sound sleep that the body has an opportunity to heal and regenerate itself.
- o Sleep in total darkness. Blackout curtains are a good idea, along with making sure digital clocks, nightlights, or other digital equipment don't introduce any light into your sleeping quarters.
- o Sleep in complete silence or to the natural sounds (not audio recordings) of nature (ocean waves, trickling water, crickets, but NOT environmental or industrial sounds of the city, and especially NOT with the TV or radio on)
- o Go to bed early enough that you don't feel a need for an "alarm" clock. If you do use an alarm clock, use one with a gentle tone or alert that nudges you awake rather than "alarming" you and startling you out of your sleep.
- o TAKE NAPS! Short naps help us feel more relaxed, full of energy, and mentally sharp and clear.
- o Incorporate regular breathing and meditation practices… Ideally daily!

Damon Givehand

APPENDIX H — THE PROSPECT OF HEALTH

We all can have HEALTH (remember the suffix TH means the accomplishment of the notion of the base, which in this case is "to heal" or "to become whole" — so we all can heal). We can starve tumors and reverse their effects by REGULARLY DETOXING, ALWAYS (without exception) EATING RIGHT, and trusting wholeheartedly that when we do these things, the body will heal itself. Not only will health be restored, excessive weight will melt away. Most people don't know this because of our education and broadcast systems, and because it generally takes a minimum of 3 months to experience and know the truth for yourself, which is longer than the majority are willing to commit. For most people, the self control it takes to DETOX without straying from a detailed regimen developed by a knowledgeable and trustworthy homeopath, naturopath, or health coach, and to ALWAYS EAT RIGHT (according to the aforementioned guidelines) for a minimum of 60 - 90 days is too great a price for them to pay, and they would rather pay with their health, peace of mind, and so-called medical "benefits" they receive as a contingency of their employment (and even a portion of their income check goes toward that, while still having to pay a "deductible" when visiting the doctor's office). Anyway, eat right and detox to keep the blood as clean as possible. Your blood and soul (soul is a substance of and in the body, believe it or not) go hand in hand. So, for the sake of your soul, never voluntarily compromise the sanctity of your blood.

As above, so below. When we master the realm of below, there is a favorable trickle up effect. In the short term, people might experience a tiny watered-down version of this when they exercise the physical body. Physical (BELOW) exercise favorably impacts the mind and emotions (ABOVE). Likewise, and in a much greater way (unimaginable for anyone who has not tried living this way for any significant amount of time), when we purify our blood, and learn to keep pleasant and joyous thoughts (as "merry" thoughts favorably affect our "Mary"/water), the same behaviors and attitudes necessary to clean the House of the body, begin to favorably affect and influence the Temple of the brain and CSF (the Temple being where the Fountain of Youth is, and the CSF being the water that springs forth and flows from The Fountain).

True knowledge comes from experience, not philosophical imaginings and fascinating conjecture.

APPENDIX I — THE EIGHT LIMBS OF YOGA

What are the eight limbs (aṣṭaṅga) of yoga as articulated in Patañjali's Yoga Sūtras?

LIMB #1. YAMA (principles governing how to interact with the world outside of ourselves)
Following are the elements making up YAMA. Practice...
Ahiṁsā = non-harming; non-injury; non-violence; harmlessness; consideration.
Satya = honesty; truthfulness; virtue.
Asteya = not stealing; not coveting; not misappropriating.
Brahmacharya = impeccable conduct; movement toward the highest; appropriate relations/relationship; retention of vital fluid.
Aparigrahāḥ = greedlessness; only accepting what is appropriate.

LIMB #2. NIYAMA (principles governing how to intra-act with ourselves)
Following are the elements that make up NIYAMA. Practice...
Śauca = purity; cleanliness (in body, speech, mind, and beyond).
Saṅtoṣa = contentment with what one has and doesn't have.
Tapaḥ = practice that reduces impurities (of the body, mind, soul, and spirit);
Svādhyāya = study that leads to knowledge of self; internal inquiry; reflection from deep within.
Iśvarapraṇidhānāni = complete and total self-surrender and submission to the infinitely intelligent divine ideal of pure awareness.

LIMB #3. ĀSANA
This is what most people in our society call "yoga" not knowing that this is but one limb of eight in Aṣṭaṅga Yoga. Āsana has to do with the postures and poses, and literally means "seat." Movement is the most effective way to increase synovial fluid production and to facilitate circulation of the lymphatic system which removes waste from the body. Āsana lengthens muscle while strengthening it, and helps make the spine flexible and strong so that you can meditate for long periods of time without the distraction of discomfort. Practice this.

Why is yogāsana such a powerful and efficient exercise?
Not only does yogāsana increase strength and flexibility AND activate the lymphatic system, yogāsana also, to some degree, easily incorporates at least 6 of the 8 limbs: niyama, asana, pranayama, pratyahara, dharana, and dhyana. The synergy of all these simultaneously during a single āsana practice, plus what it means for strength, flexibility, and lymph, makes it arguably the most powerful practice there is and sheds light on why so many have embraced "yoga" in the west, although they may not be consciously aware of these reasons — to them is just feels amazing.

If you currently have an āsana practice and are not practicing yama and niyama, begin at once to apply these as they are 1 and 2 on the list for a reason (they are foundational). If you do not currently have an āsana practice, either begin at the beginning with Yama and work your way up, OR, if you are eager to begin an āsana practice, begin with yama, niyama, AND āsana.

LIMB #4. PRĀNAYĀMA
This is the regulation of the breath and working with PRANA aka CHI (or YEU- as discussed in this book). By controlling and extending our breathing, we improve our health and mind by taking in more oxygen, AND it also helps us relax on a deep level. Prānayāma goes way deeper than this, however, but this explains it very basically on the surface. Prānayāma is its own book. A simple practice is shared in APPENDICES A and D, based on #2 BREATHE ON PURPOSE in the 9 Divine Suggestions.

LIMB #5. PRATYĀHĀRA
This is the practice of letting go of what's getting in our way (of actualizing our fullest potential), detachment, or non-attachment with things that interfere with our full development. This practice involves relinquishing vices and/or bad habits we know sabotage our well-being, but that we've "fallen" in love with, and learning to let them go without any love loss. Practice this.

LIMB #6. DHĀRANA
This is the practice of concentration, focusing the mind, and single-pointedness, the opposite of "multi-tasking" (which dis-tracts "pulls apart" the mind). This happens naturally in āsana due to the

concentration necessary to hold a pose and keep our balance. Chanting the yoga sūtras as part of a regular study practice also cultivates concentration while you learn about the mind and perception as well as how to correct the mind, which is the instrument of perception.

LIMB #7. DHYĀNA

This is the practice of meditation and expanding our awareness. If dhārana is intentional "constriction" of the mind in order to focus, think of dhyāna as intentional "dilation" of the mind in order to become aware of more. This can even show up in āsana. If we remain mindful during our āsana practices and focus on the breath as the foundation of āsana, over time, with regular practice, āsana will become a moving meditation.

LIMB #8. SAMĀDHI

This is the eighth and final limb of aṣṭaṅga, and is a prerequisite tool necessary for the attainment of the ultimate goal of Yoga, which is Kaivalyam "Freedom/Independence." I describe Samādhi (with a capital "S") as "Profound Absorption into Perfect Wholeness" (whereas samādhi with a lowercase "s" is just "profound absorption"). PERFECT WHOLENESS is the highest regard means health on every conceivable level (physical, emotional, mental, spiritual, etc...), which must be attained before Freedom (with a capital "F") can come.

ABOUT THE AUTHOR

Damon's track record reveals his deep commitment to Learning, Truth, Health, Love, and Happiness, with capital L's, T's, and H's. Despite being concurrently licensed as a mortgage broker, real estate agent, and residential appraiser in 2002, he decidedly walked away from the incredibly lucrative housing market to teach high school math in southern Florida. When he completed his graduate work in Mathematics and Education during the year of 2005, the title of his Master's thesis was 'An Indictment of Education.' Damon's path eventually led him to teaching on the collegiate level and being swept up as a nationally sought after professional development trainer for college and university professors in the area of student success and how to actively enliven curriculum and classrooms to provide optimal learning experiences.

Before transitioning out of traditional education to do the work he does now, his culminating act in that former capacity was to deliver an impassioned keynote presentation titled 'HAPPINESS: The Fuel & The Fire That Lights The Way to Greater Returns' to an international audience of more than 800 college presidents, provosts, deans, department chairs, and other leadership from nearly 50 countries worldwide.

Looking back to his classroom days, he remembers catching students' attention at the very start by saying "I hate school" when introducing himself. At least one student in every class would always ask, "Then why do you teach, Mr. G?" His reply: Because I LOVE LEARNING and teaching you all to do the most important math there is — YOUR LIFE! From there, the stage would be set! Even when teaching math, Damon always weaved health and serious life lessons into his discussions, vowing never to tell students what to think but show and teach them how to think to live the highest quality life possible. When training professors, Damon was always careful to say "Don't try this at home."

Outside and beyond government sanctioned education, Damon's growing interest and enthusiasm in yoga over the years has led him to completing multiple certifications: 200-hr Ashtanga Yoga/Vinyasa Flow, 500-hr Viniyoga, and at the time of this writing he's on his way to completing an Advanced 1000-hr Yoga Therapist Certification, all of which equip him to teach yoga enthusiasts the profound practical philosophy of Patañjali's Yoga Sūtras (which he does now).

Today, Damon enjoys working alongside his soul mate, best friend, lover, life partner, and wife, Kiala, as Cofounder of Healing Arts Creativity & Empowerment Studio in Pensacola, FL — a space created for anyone hungry to learn the art of healing, becoming whole, and actualizing their fullest potential — which can be found online at HealingArtsCreativeStudio.com. Together, Damon and Kiala teach the 12 Radical Intentions™ for living The R.I.C.H. Life™, a practical philosophy for realizing the fruits of a life Radically Intent on Cultivating Happiness.

Damon is also the author of OPTIMUM HEALTH MINDSET (OHM): How to Think to Undo Fat, Maximize Your Vitality, and Never Get Sick Again.

Made in the USA
Lexington, KY
06 March 2019